BUSINESS ASSOCIATIONS

OBJECTIVE

JENS C. DAMMANN

The University of Texas School of Law

Exam Pro ®

WEST
ACADEMIC
PUBLISHING

Exam Pro Series is a trademark registered in the U.S. Patent and Trademark Office.

© 2016 LEG, Inc. d/b/a West Academic
    444 Cedar Street, Suite 700
    St. Paul, MN 55101
    1-877-888-1330

West, West Academic Publishing, and West Academic are trademarks of West Publishing Corporation, used under license.

Printed in the United States of America

ISBN: 978-1-62810-194-2

Preface

The multiple choice questions and answers in this volume are designed to help students understand and review central concepts in the law of business associations.

To the extent that the questions in this book deal with corporate or LLC law, they focus on the law of Delaware. This is no accident. Delaware is home to more than half of all publicly traded corporations in the United States, and it is also the destination of choice for large privately held corporations and limited liability companies. Hence, students taking a course in the law of business associations will typically end up spending much of their time studying Delaware law.

To give readers a better idea of where they stand, I have ranked questions by difficulty. One star means that a question is relatively easy; often, such questions can be answered by carefully reading the relevant statutory provision(s). Two stars mean that the question is somewhat more difficult. Most questions fall into this category. A few questions are sufficiently complex that I have marked them with three stars.

By way of a rough guideline, answering a one-star question should not take more than 2 to 3 minutes. Answering a question marked with two stars should not take more than 4 to 5 minutes, and answering a question with three stars should not take more than 6 minutes.

Jens C. Dammann

November 2015

Table of Contents

BUSINESS ASSOCIATIONS

PART 1
QUESTIONS

CHAPTER 1
AGENCY LAW

Facts for Question 1 (*)

When Jennifer, a famous actress, walks by a jewelry store, she notices a beautiful ring in the window. Unfortunately, she does not have her credit card with her. Later in the day, she tells a friend of hers, Ben, about the ring, saying: "I would love to have that ring, but don't have the time to go to the jewelry store tomorrow." Ben offers to buy the ring on her behalf. Jennifer is delighted and tells him: "You are such a darling. Just make sure that you make it clear that you are buying the ring on my behalf. After all, I am famous, and the storeowner will probably sell it at a lower price if he knows I'm the buyer. Also, you don't have to pay the storeowner immediately. Just tell him he will be paid by the end of the week." Ben agrees to do this. Later, however, he thinks the matter over and comes to the conclusion that he will probably be able to buy the ring more cheaply if he does not mention Jennifer's involvement. The next day, therefore, Ben goes to the jewelry store and buys the ring at a price of $1000 without ever mentioning that he is acting on someone else's behalf. George is the owner and operator of the store. Ben receives the ring after promising that George will get the money by the end of the week. Which of the following statements is most correct?

(A) Jennifer is an undisclosed principal.

(B) Jennifer is an unidentified principal.

(C) Jennifer is a disclosed principal.

(D) Ben has overstepped his actual authority, but has acted with apparent authority.

Facts for Question 2 (*)

Peter sends his employee Raphael to buy a pizza at Casey's Italian restaurant. Raphael tells Casey that he, Raphael, is acting for Peter. Secretly, though, Raphael wants the contract to be between himself and Casey. Casey, taking Raphael at his word, assumes that the latter is acting on behalf of Peter. Has a contract been formed between Casey and Peter?

(A) Yes, because Raphael acted with actual authority and because Casey reasonably assumed that Raphael was Peter's agent.

(B) Yes, because Raphael acted with apparent authority and because Casey reasonably assumed that Raphael was Peter's agent.

(C) No, because Raphael did not have authority.

(D) No, because Raphael acted for himself rather than for Peter.

Facts for Question 3 (*)

Arturo tells his employee Charlie to rent a Ferrari for him from a nearby car rental enterprise. As soon as Charlie has left, Arturo calls the relevant car rental enterprise, states his name, and says: "I have sent my employee Charlie over to rent a car for me. He can rent any car as long as it is luxurious." The employee in charge at the car rental enterprise concludes that Charlie has authority to rent a luxurious car for Arturo, no matter the brand. As it happens, the car rental no longer has Ferraris in store. Therefore, Charlie decides to rent a Bentley instead. Is Arturo bound to the contract, and, if so, why?

    (A) Arturo is bound to the contract because Charlie acted with actual authority.

    (B) Arturo is bound to the contract because Charlie acted with apparent authority.

    (C) Arturo is bound to the contract because the contract was ratified.

    (D) Arturo is bound to the contract because of estoppel.

Facts for Question 4 (*)

Nyusha, who owns and operates a ranch, tells her employee Dylan to go see Marcus, a horse trader, and inquire if he has any good horses to sell. Nyusha also tells Dylan not to buy any animals yet, but simply to report back on what Marcus might be offering. Dylan goes to Marcus and tells him that she is looking to buy some horses for Nyusha. He offers her a white horse for $20,000 and a black horse for $25,000. Disregarding her instructions, Dylan buys both horses in Nyusha's name as part of a single transaction for a total price of $45,000. The contract is in writing and signed by both Dylan and Nyusha. Dylan purchased the horses because she is convinced that Nyusha will be o.k. with the deal. When she reports back to Nyusha, the latter is shocked. Nyusha then visits Marcus, tells him that Dylan was not allowed to buy anything and also says: "I like the black horse, so I will pay you the $25,000, but I am not taking the white horse." Marcus, who has another willing buyer for both horses, tells Nyusha to "get lost." Does Nyusha have any rights against Marcus?

    (A) Yes, because Dylan acted with actual authority.

    (B) Yes, because Dylan acted with apparent authority.

    (C) Yes, because Nyusha ratified the contract.

    (D) No.

Facts for Question 5 (**)

Fatima owns and operates a bookstore called "Best Books." When she has to leave town for a month to take care of her sick mother, she asks her friend Maya to fill in for her while she is gone. Maya agrees. On the first day that Maya takes care of the store, she notices that the store does not have any books in stock by the popular author Ronny Miegel. Therefore, Maya calls the publisher, George, and, making it clear that she acts for Best Books, orders 10 new copies of Miegel's most recent book for a total price of $300. The publisher assumes that Maya is the owner and operator of Best Books. The books are promptly delivered. Unbeknownst to Maya, Fatima does not like Miegel, and when she returns after a month and learns that Maya has bought 10 copies of Miegel's most recent book, Fatima calls George, explains to him that Maya was just filling in and tells him that she, Fatima, "is not o.k. with the purchase" and "won't be held liable for the books." Are Maya and/or Fatima liable to George?

    (A) Fatima is liable to George, and so is Maya.

    (B) Fatima is liable to George, but Maya is not.

    (C) Fatima is not liable to George, but Maya is.

    (D) Fatima is not liable to George, and neither is Maya.

Facts for Question 6 (**)

Genevieve owns and operates a garage. She has seven mechanics working for her, including Kenji, who has only recently become Genevieve's employee. Every morning at 6 a.m., the mechanics come in and the work begins. Genevieve then assigns Kenji what she calls "the first job of the day"—getting breakfast for everyone from a nearby fast food store. Kenji originally tried to refuse, but Genevieve pointed out that she was not only giving him money for the purchase, but also reimbursing him for the cost of the gas. She also noted that having one employee purchase breakfast for the whole group saved time and allowed the others to get more work done. One day, when Kenji is sent off to get breakfast, he is still tired and negligently damages a car belonging to a person named Travis while trying to park his own. Who is liable for the damage?

    (A) Kenji is liable to Travis, but Genevieve is not.

    (B) Genevieve is liable to Travis, but Kenji is not.

    (C) Genevieve is liable to Travis, and so is Kenji.

    (D) Genevieve is not liable to Travis, and neither is Kenji.

Facts for Question 7 (**)

Carl is a wealthy landowner. One fine day, he learns that one of the neighboring ranches will be auctioned and decides to try and buy it. Unfortunately for Carl, the auction will take place on July 1, when Carl will be spending his summer vacation in Europe. He therefore instructs his secretary, Gino, to attend the auction in Carl's name and bid up to $5,000,000 for the property. Gino has never before bought any land in Carl's name, but he has frequently undertaken minor purchases for Carl such as buying flowers for Carl's garden or toys for Carl's children.

On the day of the auction, there are several bidders who try to purchase the ranch in question, and in the heat of the bidding war, Gino gets carried away. He wins the auction, but only after bidding $5,500,000. After realizing that he has exceeded the limit imposed by Carl, Gino is panicked. At that moment, another bidder, Louis, walks up to Gino, and offers to buy a particular piece of land that forms part of the ranch for $500,000. Gino, explicitly acting in Carl's name, gladly accepts, and they both sign a written sales contract to this effect. Because the relevant part of the land amounts to only 5% of the overall area of the ranch, Gino is sure that Carl will not mind.

Two weeks later, Carl returns from this vacation. Gino confesses that he has acquired the ranch for $5,500,000, but forgets to mention that he also sold part of the property. Carl is shocked but says: "Well, what's done is done, I would rather overpay than not get the ranch at all." He then pays the $5,500,000, and the property is transferred to Carl. A week later, Louis contacts Carl and points out that he, Louis, has bought part of the ranch. Carl flatly tells him that he does not feel bound by the contract signed by Gino and Louis. Which of the following statements is correct?

(A) Neither the contract in the amount of $5,500,000 nor the contract in the amount of $500,000 binds Carl.

(B) The contract in the amount of $5,500,000 binds Carl, whereas the contract in the amount of $500,000 does not bind Carl.

(C) The contract in the amount of $500,000 binds Carl, whereas the contract in the amount of $5,500,000 does not bind Carl.

(D) Both contracts bind Carl.

Facts for Question 8 (**)

Gerard is an eccentric billionaire living in Big City. One day, Jeff, one of Gerard's personal assistants, reports to him that a scam artist named Joe seems to be making the rounds in Big City. Joe's modus operandi is as follows: Joe visits luxury car dealerships and pretends to be working for Gerard. Acting in Gerard's name, Joe then acquires luxury cars and drives them away, promising that Gerard will pay the within the next 30 days. So far, no one has realized that Joe is a scam artist except Jeff and Gerard. Jeff points out that Joe has already defrauded six of Big City's seven luxury car dealerships, and Jeff proposes warning the seventh so that it does not fall victim to the same trick. However, Gerard replies: "No, this is far too amusing. Let's just wait and see if that store is as dumb as the others." Two days later, Joe visits the seventh luxury car dealership which is owned and operated by Susan. Susan has already heard that Joe has been buying luxury cars for Gerard, but does not realize that Joe is a scam artist. Therefore, she readily agrees to sell a new Mercedes at a price of $120,000. They both sign the contract, and as usual, Joe does so in Gerard's name. Then Joe drives away in the Mercedes and is never heard of again.

After a while, Susan asks Gerard to pay for the Mercedes. However, Gerard refuses, pointing out that Joe was just a scam artist abusing Gerard's good name. Who, if anyone, is liable to Susan?

(A) Both Joe and Gerard are liable to Susan.

(B) Joe is liable, but Gerard is not.

(C) Gerard is liable to Susan, but Joe is not.

(D) Neither Joe nor Gerard is liable to Susan.

CHAPTER 2
PARTNERSHIP LAW

Facts for Question 1 (*)

On January 1, Maria and Reuben decide to open a law firm ("Maria & Reuben Law Partners"). They agree that the firm will open its doors to the public on January 15. On January 5, Reuben, acting in the name of "Maria & Reuben Law Partners," calls Peter, a printer, and orders 5000 business cards. When, on January 6, Maria learns of this order, she promptly calls Peter and tells him that she does not approve of the purchase and "won't be held responsible." Peter insists that both Reuben and Maria are liable to him. Can Peter hold Maria and/or Reuben personally liable?

(A) Reuben and Maria are jointly and severally liable to Peter.

(B) Reuben is liable to Peter, but Maria is not.

(C) Maria is liable to Peter, but Reuben is not.

(D) Maria is not liable to Peter, and neither is Reuben.

Facts for Question 2 (**)

On January 1, Rosalind and Viola agree to launch a repertory theater company together. Under the written "theater company agreement," which they both sign, each of them shall get 50% of the profits. On January 10, Rosalind negligently causes a traffic accident while delivering some promotional materials, a task that she undertakes several times a week. As a result of that accident, a pedestrian, Will, is injured and incurs medical costs in the amount of $100,000. On January 15, Rosalind and Viola sign an agreement with Cordelia according to which Cordelia "joins the firm." The agreement also provides that henceforth, Rosalind, Viola, and Cordelia shall each be entitled to one third of the profits made by the theater company. In the following, the firm sells off its assets to be able to pay Will, but even after all assets are sold, only $60,000 out of the $100,000 have been paid. Are any of the three entrepreneurs (Rosalind, Viola, and Cordelia) personally liable to Will with respect to the remaining $40,000?

(A) Rosalind is liable to Will, but Viola and Cordelia are not.

(B) Rosalind and Viola are jointly and severally liable to Will, but Cordelia is not.

(C) Rosalind, Viola, and Cordelia are jointly and severally liable to Will.

(D) Neither Rosalind nor Viola nor Cordelia is liable to Will.

Facts for Question 3 (*)

In January 2013, Alexei and his brothers Ivan and Dmitri start a comic book store together in a state that has adopted the Revised Uniform

Partnership Act. The three brothers all sign an agreement under which Alexei and Ivan each get 30 percent of the profits, whereas Dmitri gets the remaining 40 percent. The agreement does not mention losses. The partnership agreement further provides that each of the three brothers shall contribute $15,000 in cash to the firm. In February 2013, all three partners pay their promised contributions. In 2013, the firm incurs a net loss in the amount of $10,000. In 2014, the partnership makes a net profit in the amount of $100,000. Throughout the two years, the partnership never pays any money to Alexei or Ivan. By contrast, the partnership pays Dmitri $5,000 on December 1, 2013, and another $2,000 on December 1, 2014. What do the partners' accounts look like at the end of 2014?

(A) Each of the three brothers' accounts shows a plus of $72,000.

(B) The accounts of Alexei and Ivan show a plus of $42,000. Dmitri's account shows a plus of $51,000.

(C) The accounts of Alexei and Ivan show a plus of $42,000. Dmitri's account shows a plus of $44,000.

(D) None of the answers above is correct.

Facts for Question 4 (*)

Fred, George and Percy are partners in a partnership that owns and operates a store for fine foods. Under the partnership agreement, only Fred and George are to manage the business, whereas Percy has no right or duty to participate in the firm's management; his sole role is to contribute money. On Sunday, January 13, 2014, Percy visits the store and notices that the roof of the shop is leaking. He tries to contact Fred and George but cannot reach either one. Therefore, Percy calls a repairman. The repairman comes right away and fixes the roof, but Percy has to pay him $150. Percy uses his own personal credit card because he does not have access to the partnership's bank account. Can Percy demand to be reimbursed?

(A) Yes, but only to the extent that the partnership is unjustly enriched.

(B) Yes, and that is true regardless of whether the elements of an unjust enrichment claim are present.

(C) No, because Percy was not entitled to interfere with the management of the partnership.

(D) None of the answer choices above is correct.

Facts for Question 5 (*)

Fred, George and Percy are partners in a partnership that owns and operates a store for fine foods. Early in 2014, the brothers buy a car for the enterprise. One day, after the shop has closed, Percy takes the car for a ride to pick up his girlfriend Penelope. He mentioned this to George in advance, and George said he was o.k. with it. Neither George nor Percy notified Fred. Has Percy violated his duties as a partner?

(A) Yes, because Fred did not consent to the use of the car.

(B) Yes, and this would be true even if Fred, too, had consented to the use of the car.

(C) No, because two of the three partners consented to the use of the car.

(D) No, and this would be true even if George had not consented to the use of the car.

Facts for Question 6 (*)

Fred, George and Percy are partners in a partnership that owns and operates a store for fine foods. Soon, the brothers find themselves arguing over whether to buy caviar for the store. Percy has ethical objections to this purchase. Fred and George are in favor of it. Do Fred and George violate their duties towards Percy if they buy some caviar on behalf of the partnership?

(A) Yes, because Percy did not consent to the purchase.

(B) No, because two out of three partners favored the purchase.

(C) No, in fact, even if two partners had opposed the purchase, the third partner could have purchased the caviar for the partnership without violating his duties.

(D) None of the answer choices above is correct.

Facts for Question 7 (*)

Fred, George and Percy are partners in a partnership that owns and operates a record store. As it turns out, Percy, who is a rather annoying fellow, scares off most of the customers. Therefore, George and Fred tell him: "Look, you can remain a co-owner of the enterprise, but leave the running of the business to us. You are way too embarrassing." Does Percy have to comply?

(A) Yes, because questions pertaining to the running of the business can be decided by a simple majority of the partners.

(B) Yes, but only because George and Fred had a legitimate reason to exclude Percy from the running of the business.

(C) No, because every partner has a right to participate in the management of the firm.

(D) None of the answer choices above is correct.

Facts for Question 8 (*)

Fred, George and Percy are partners in a partnership that owns and operates a car parts store. Ginevra, their younger sister, wants to join the enterprise. She has an MBA from a top business school. Contrary to Percy's wishes, Fred and George enter into a written agreement with Ginevra according to which she becomes a co-owner of the enterprise. Does the partnership now include Ginevra as a partner?

(A) Yes, because the admission of new partners can be decided by a majority of the partners.

(B) Yes, but only because Percy could not, in good faith, refuse to admit Ginevra as a partner.

(C) No, because the admission of new partners requires the consent of all the existing partners.

(D) None of the answer choices above is correct.

Facts for Question 9 (*)

Homer, Ovid and Lucan are partners in a partnership that owns and operates a bicycle store. The partnership is governed by the RUPA. In March 2014, Homer tells Lucan that he wants to see the firm's books. Lucan refuses. He points out, truthfully, that the written agreement between the partners contains the following clause: "Lucan will function as the firm's bookkeeper. No one else shall have access to the firm's books." Does Homer have a right to see the books anyhow? Can Homer demand that the books also be shown to his attorney Horace?

(A) Homer has a right to see the books, and he can also demand that the books also be shown to his attorney, Horace.

(B) Homer has a right to see the books, but he cannot demand that the books also be shown to his attorney, Horace.

(C) Homer has no right to see the books, but he can demand that the books be shown to his attorney, Horace.

(D) Homer has no right to see the books, and he cannot demand that the books be shown to his attorney Horace.

Facts for Question 10 (*)

Thelma and Louise run a store that sells exclusively firecrackers. Effective January 1, 2013, the state legislature enacts a statute prohibiting the sale of firecrackers for safety reasons. However, only thirty days later, the legislature repeals that statute. Thelma and Louise want to know what the legal status of their firm is. Assuming that the firm is governed by the RUPA, has the partnership been dissolved and is it still dissolved?

(A) The partnership was dissolved when the first statute became effective, but, due to the second statute, we treat the partnership as though it had never been dissolved.

(B) The partnership was dissolved by the first statute and remains dissolved despite the second statute.

(C) The partnership was dissolved by the first statute, but was newly formed when the second statute went into effect.

(D) The partnership was never dissolved in the first place, and this would be true even if the second statute had not been enacted.

Facts for Question 11 (*)

On January 1, 2013, Larry, Moe, and Bearle sign a written "partnership agreement" according to which they shall form, own, and operate a book store. The agreement provides that each of the three shall receive one third of the profits. The agreement also contains the following provisions:

"This partnership shall last ten years. However, any partner can be expelled at any time if the other partners unanimously agree that he or she should be expelled."

Throughout the year 2013, Larry complains regularly about the state of the firm's business. Moe and Bearle are more optimistic, and they grow tired of Larry's constant complaints. Therefore, on December 31, 2013, when Larry, Moe, and Bearle meet, Moe and Bearle vote to expel Larry. Which, if any, of the following statements is correct?

(A) Larry has been dissociated from the partnership, but the other two partners violated their fiduciary duties when they expelled Larry.

(B) Larry has not been dissociated from the partnership, but only because the other two partners violated their fiduciary duties when they expelled Larry.

(C) Larry has not been dissociated from the partnership because partners cannot be expelled without good cause, and this rule is mandatory.

(D) Larry has been dissociated from the partnership, and the other partners did not violate their fiduciary duties.

Facts for Question 12 (*)

What sorts of entities can be partners in a partnership?

(A) A natural person, a corporation, a trust, and a partnership.

(B) A natural person, a corporation, a trust, but not a partnership.

(C) A natural person, a corporation, a partnership, but not a trust.

(D) A natural person, a trust, a partnership, but not a corporation.

Facts for Question 13 (**)

On January 1, 2014, Brad, Tom, and Sandy agree that they will start a bakery together and that each of them will get one third of the profits. They also agree, without putting it into writing, that the firm shall go on for "at least 10 months even if business is horrible." On January 15, the bakery opens its doors to the public.

Soon afterwards, the three have a bitter disagreement about whether to use solely organic flour or non-organic flour as well. During a heated discussion on January 20, 2014, Tom says: "This firm is finished, let's shut the whole thing down." Brad replies: "Oh yeah? Fine with me, this business is over." Sandy simply says: "I agree." On January 25, Sandy dies in a traffic accident. On January 30, Brad dies of a heart attack. Has the partnership been dissolved and, if so, when?

(A) The partnership was dissolved on January 20, 2014.

(B) The partnership was dissolved on January 25, 2014

(C) The partnership was dissolved on January 30, 2014

(D) The partnership has not been dissolved.

Facts for Question 14 (**)

Four once-famous musicians, Mick, Keith, Charlie, and Ron, leave their retirement to undertake a four months comeback tour that shall take them across all continents. They agree that they will stay together at least as long as it takes to complete the comeback tour, and they also agree that each of them shall get one quarter of the profits from the tour. However, only two weeks into the tour, Keith surprisingly dies after falling off a palm tree. Mick wants to go on nonetheless, but Charlie and Ron declare that they want to wind up the business. One week later, Ron dies of a drug overdose. Has the partnership been dissolved and, if so, when? Assume that the state whose law governs this case has adopted the RUPA.

(A) The partnership was dissolved when Keith died.

(B) The partnership was dissolved when Charlie and Ron declared that they wanted to wind up the business.

(C) The partnership was dissolved when Ron died.

(D) The partnership has not been dissolved.

Facts for Question 15 (**)

Giles and Anya own and operate a magic shop together. The statement of partnership authority that they have filed makes it clear that under the partnership agreement neither Anya nor Giles is allowed to enter into contracts for more than $400. One day, Giles, claiming to act for the partnership, enters into a contract with Willow according to which the partnership will pay Willow $450 for two secondhand spell books. Assume that Willow did not know and was not notified of the restriction on Giles' authority to act for the partnership. Furthermore, assume that the case is governed by the RUPA. Has the purchase created a partnership liability?

(A) Yes, because the partnership agreement cannot limit a partner's authority to enter into transactions in the ordinary course of business.

(B) Yes, because the statement of partnership authority cannot be invoked to Willow's detriment.

(C) No, because the partnership agreement limited the authority of the partners. This would be true even if no statement of partnership authority had been filed.

(D) No, but only because of the statement of partnership authority.

Facts for Question 16 (**)

Harry and Sally decide to start an enterprise selling hats. They both sign a "business agreement." According to that agreement, Harry is to contribute $50,000 and will receive 20% of the profits, but he will not to bear any of the losses. Sally is to get 80% of the profits. In addition, Sally is to bear all the losses and do all the work. The written agreement also stipulates that Sally can decide, without Harry's consent, to let the business obtain loans up to $200,000. The written agreement between Harry and Sally furthermore contains the following clause: "This is not a partnership, but a joint venture. Only Sally will be liable to third parties."

Subsequently, Harry contributes the promised $50,000. Nonetheless, the firm soon runs out of cash. Harry makes it clear to Sally that he, Harry, does not want the firm to take on any loans. Furthermore, Harry contacts all local banks and lets them know that he has instructed Sally "not to take on any loans for the joint venture." On May 1, 2013, however, Sally, acting in the name of the enterprise, requests and obtains a loan from a local bank in the amount of $10,000. The firm's business is not going well, and by March 2014, the firm no longer has any assets. Assume that the applicable state law is identical to the RUPA (1997). Can the bank hold Harry personally liable for all or at least part of the $10,000?

(A) Yes, Harry is personally liable to the bank for the full $10,000.

(B) Yes, Harry is personally liable to the bank, but only in the amount of $5,000.

(C) No, Harry is not personally liable because the firm was not a partnership.

(D) No, Harry is not personally liable because the bank knew that Harry was opposed to the loan.

Facts for Question 17 (**)

On January 1, 2013, Bruce, Arnold, Denzel, Jackie, and Sylvester start a restaurant together. They have agreed to keep the firm running until December 31, 2022. However, on January 1, 2014, Bruce dies in a high-speed car chase. At a meeting on January 2, 2014, Denzel and Jackie want to keep going, but Arnold and Sylvester express their wish to wind up the firm's business. On January 3, 2014, Jackie buys twenty new restaurant tables from Tom. Tom has been familiar with the restaurant since it was formed. Moreover, at the moment of the purchase, Tom does not know that Bruce has died, or that Arnold and Sylvester have expressed their wish to wind up the firm's business. As no news of the events at the restaurant was mentioned in any newspaper, Tom could not have been expected to know more than he does about the matter. Does the contract with Tom still bind the partnership? Assume that the RUPA is the applicable law.

(A) The contract with Tom does not bind the partnership because the partnership has been dissolved and therefore no longer exists.

(B) The contract with Tom does not bind the partnership. Even though the partnership did exist at the moment of the transaction, Jackie did not have the authority to bind the partnership.

(C) The contract with Tom binds the partnership but only because Tom did not know, and did not have reason to know, of the partnership's dissolution.

(D) The contract with Tom binds the partnership, and the partnership has not been dissolved.

Facts for Question 18 (**)

Dolly, Emmylou, Loretta and Patsy own and operate a restaurant together. Each of them has contributed $10,000 to the restaurant. They have made an agreement regarding neither the duration of their enterprise, nor the matter of how the restaurant's profits will be distributed. However, they have agreed that the partnership shall not be dissolved by the dissociation of a partner as long as two or more partners remain. The restaurant has only once made a distribution to the partners, at which time each partner received $10,000.

On January 1, 2013, Dolly tells her fellow entrepreneurs that she has decided to take up a career as a country singer and that she has no more interest in running a restaurant. "In short," she says, "I am out, effective immediately." The next day, Dolly consults her lawyer to find out how much (if any) money she can expect in exchange for her partnership interest. Including all assets and liabilities, the restaurant has a going concern value of 1,000,000. Its liquidation value is $400,000. Assume that the state in which the restaurant is located has adopted the RUPA. Which of the following statements is most correct?

(A) Dolly cannot expect to be paid anything because the agreement does not mention any right to payment on dissociation.

(B) Dolly can only expect to be paid the value of her original contribution in the amount of $10,000.

(C) Dolly can expect to be paid $100,000.

(D) Dolly can expect to be paid $250,000.

Facts for Question 19 (**)

Hank, Conway, Buck and Johnny own and operate a restaurant together. On January 1, 2012, Hank persuades his fellow entrepreneurs that the firm should obtain a loan of $100,000. The next day, Hank signs a loan agreement on behalf of the firm with Bank Corp., a local bank. According to the loan agreement, the firm gets a loan in the amount of $100,000 which it has to pay back on December 1, 2013. On January 3, 2012, Buck tells Hank, Conway and Johnny that he no longer enjoys running a restaurant and that he wants out, effective immediately. The others give him their blessing and the firm purchases "Buck's stake in the firm" for $100,000. Two days later Buck takes a plane to Mexico where he plans to open a radio station.

In December 2012, it becomes clear that the restaurant cannot repay the loan on time. Therefore, Hank calls Bank Corp. and points out that because Buck has left the firm and received money in exchange for his stake in the firm, the restaurant is a little low on cash. After some back and forth, Hank and Bank Corp. agree that instead of paying back the $100,000 on January 1, 2013, the restaurant will pay back $110,000 on January 1, 2014. However, business gets worse over time, and by January 1, 2014 the restaurant has no assets left and cannot pay Bank Corp. Can Bank Corp. hold Buck liable with respect to some or all of the $110,000? Assume that the state where the restaurant is located has adopted the RUPA.

(A) Buck is liable to Bank Corp. in the amount of $110,000.

(B) Buck is liable to Bank Corp., but only in the amount of $100,000.

(C) Buck is liable to Bank Corp., but only in the amount of $52,500.

(D) Bank Corp. cannot hold Buck personally liable.

Facts for Question 20 (**)

Charlotte, Emily, Anne, and Branwell own and operate a vegetarian restaurant together. On January 1, 2013, Charlotte dissociates from the partnership. On January 4, 2013, the partnership files a statement of dissociation which contains information about Charlotte's dissociation. Elizabeth has long supplied tofu to the partnership's restaurant and, based on her previous dealings with the partnership, believes that Charlotte is a still a partner. Elizabeth does not know, and has no reason to know, that Charlotte has left the partnership. On January 6, 2013, Charlotte calls Elizabeth and, acting in the name of the partnership, buys 60 pounds of premium pressed tofu for a total price of $400. Charlotte takes the tofu with her and promises that Elizabeth will be paid the same week. Then Charlotte boards a ship to South America and is never seen again. It furthermore turns out that the partnership does not have any assets. Elizabeth now wants to hold Emily liable, because she is the only one of the partners who has any assets. Assume that the state whose law is applicable has adopted the RUPA. Which of the following statements is most correct?

(A) Emily is liable for the full $400, but only because Elizabeth did not know or have notice that Charlotte had left the partnership.

(B) Emily is liable for the full $400, and the same would be true if Elizabeth, at the time the contract was formed, had known about Charlotte's dissociation.

(C) Emily is not liable with respect to the $400, but only because of the statement of dissociation.

(D) Emily is not liable with respect to the $400, and this would have been true even if no statement of dissociation had been filed.

Facts for Question 21 (***)

Will, Jill, Hester, Chester, Peter, Polly, Tim, Tom, Mary, Larry, and Clarinda own and operate a restaurant together. On January 1, Will, Jill, Hester, Chester, Peter, Polly, Tim, Tom, Mary, and Larry discover that Clarinda has repeatedly stolen small sums of money from the restaurant, totaling about $1500 over two years. They therefore resolve, against Clarinda's will, to expel her from the partnership with immediate effect. The partnership agreement is silent on the question of whether partners can be expelled. On January 2, Larry is involved in a car accident and suffers serious brain injuries. On January 10, a court appoints Will as Larry's legal guardian. On January 12, Tom gets married. On January 14, Tim dies in a car accident. On January 16, Polly files for bankruptcy. On January 18, the remaining partners discover that Peter has secretly passed on the restaurant's secret recipes to a competing restaurant in exchange for $10,000. Assume that the state in which the restaurant is located has adopted the RUPA. Which of the following statements is most correct?

    (A) The partnership was dissolved before January 20, but not before January 10.

    (B) The partnership was dissolved before January 10.

    (C) On January 20, the partnership still has not been dissolved, and the remaining partners include Will, Jill, Hester, Chester, Peter, Tom, Mary, and Clarinda, but no one else.

    (D) On January 20, the partnership still has not been dissolved, and the remaining partners include Will, Jill, Hester, Chester, Peter, Tom, and Mary, but no one else.

Facts for Question 22 (**)

Chandler and Joey own and operate a bicycle store together. According to their written "business agreement", each of them is entitled to 50% of the profits. The agreement does not mention losses. On January 1, Chandler causes a traffic accident while driving to a supplier to pick up some new bikes. In causing the accident, Chandler acted with simple negligence. As a result of the accident, Ross, a pedestrian, is injured and subsequently incurs medical costs in the amount of $1000. Because the partnership does not currently have any money in its account, Chandler pays the $1000 dollar by check from his personal account. Can he demand to be reimbursed by the firm?

    (A) Chandler has no right to be reimbursed, because the agreement between Joey and Chandler does not mention any claim to reimbursement.

    (B) Chandler has no right to be reimbursed, because the accident was due to his own negligence.

    (C) Chandler has no right to be reimbursed, because the partnership was never liable to Ross in the first place.

    (D) Yes, Chandler has the right to be reimbursed by the firm.

Facts for Question 23 (**)

On January 1, 2013, Lisa, Mary, and Nora all sign a written agreement according to which they will open a bookstore together. According to the agreement, each of them shall receive one third of the profits. The agreement also provides that each of them shall make a contribution in the amount of $150.

On January 2, 2013, Lisa, Mary, and Nora each pay the promised $150.

On January 15, 2013, the bookstore opens its doors to the public.

On January 17, 2013, Lisa, is putting books onto shelves in the bookstore. Acting with simple negligence, she bumps into an elderly customer, Mark. This causes Mark to fall and hurt his leg. As a result, the customer, Mark, has to receive medical treatment at a cost of $100.

On January 18, 2013, Lisa, Mary and Nora enter into a written agreement with Alma, according to which Alma joins the firm in exchange for making a contribution in the amount of $150. Alma pays the $150 the same day. The agreement with Alma also provides that, henceforth, each of the four (Lisa, Mary, Nora, and Alma) shall receive one fourth of the profits.

On January 20, 2013, Mark goes to the store and demands $100 to cover the medical expenses he has incurred as a result of hurting his leg. Regarding the $100 demanded by Mark, which, if any, of the following statements is true?

(A) Lisa, Mary, Nora, and Alma are jointly and severally liable. The partnership itself is not liable because it is not a legal entity distinct from the partners.

(B) The partnership is liable to Mark. Furthermore Lisa, Mary, Nora and Alma are jointly and severally liable for the partnership's obligation to Mark.

(C) Lisa, Mary, and Nora are jointly and severally liable. The partnership itself is not liable because it is not a legal entity distinct from the partners. Alma is not personally liable to Mark.

(D) The partnership is liable to Mark. Furthermore Lisa, Mary, and Nora are jointly and severally liable for the partnership's obligation to Mark. Alma is not personally liable to Mark.

Facts for Question 24 (**)

On January 1, 2013, Richard, Clive, and Owen open a bookstore together. According to a written agreement, which they all sign the same day, each of them gets one third of the profits. Furthermore, the agreement specifies that the "business shall continue for exactly ten years and shall then dissolve automatically." On January 3, 2013, Richard dies in a car accident. He has no heirs. On January 5, 2013, Clive dies of a heart attack. His only heir is his wife Mary. On January 7, 2013, Mary meets Owen, and they both agree to "carry on the business together as co-owners." Assume that the applicable state law on partnerships is identical to the RUPA. Which of the following statements is correct?

(A) On January 1, 2013, Richard, Clive, and Owen formed a partnership. That partnership was dissolved on January 3, when Richard died.

(B) On January 1, 2013, Richard, Clive, and Owen formed a partnership. That partnership was dissolved on January 5, when Clive died.

(C) On January 1, 2013, Richard, Clive, and Owen formed a partnership. That partnership was not dissolved by Richard's death, and it was not dissolved by Clive's death either. However, it was dissolved and replaced by a new partnership on January 7, when Mary and Owen decided to carry on the business as co-owners.

(D) On January 1, 2013, Richard, Clive, and Owen formed a partnership. That partnership was not dissolved by Richard's death, and it was not dissolved by Clive's death either. Nor was it dissolved on January

7, 2013. However, it will be dissolved automatically on December 31, 2023.

Facts for Question 25 (***)

Pam and Joe are co-owners of a small soccer equipment store ("Soccer-Land") that they operate together in Los Angeles. According to an oral agreement, Pam has authority to purchase all kinds of goods for the firm, not just those goods that are normally sold in a soccer equipment store. Moreover, on January 1, 2000, a statement of partnership authority is filed according to which Pam has authority to purchase all kinds of goods for the firm, not just those goods that are normally sold in a soccer equipment store. On February 2, 2000, Joe and Pam agree that henceforth, Pam shall only have authority to purchase soccer balls for the firm.

On January 3, 2010, Pam, acting in the name of "Soccer-Land", calls Robert, an antiquities dealer. Robert happens to know Soccer-Land, because his children purchase all their soccer equipment there. Pam, acting in the name of "Soccer-Land" purchases a collection of antique violins at a price of $1,500,000 from Robert. Robert delivers the violins immediately, but is not paid. Pamela bought the violins because she thought they were a "splendid deal." Joe knew nothing of the purchase.

At the time of the purchase, Robert does not know about—and has not received notification of—the statement of partnership authority. Nor is he aware (or has any reason to be aware) of the agreement according to which only Pam shall have authority to purchase only soccer balls for the firm, and he (Robert) has not received any notification of that agreement either. Assume that the case is governed by the RUPA.

Is Joe personally liable with respect to the $1,500,000?

(A) Yes, but only because Robert could rely on the statement of partnership authority.

(B) Yes, and the same would be true if no statement of partnership authority had been filed.

(C) No, because a statement of partnership authority can never be invoked to the disadvantage of the partnership except in certain cases involving real estate.

(D) No, because the purchase was not for apparently carrying on in the ordinary course the firm's business.

CHAPTER 3
CORPORATE LAW

Facts for Question 1 (*)

Under Delaware law, which of the following elements does not necessarily have to be included in a corporation's certificate of incorporation?

(A) The address of the corporation's registered office in Delaware.

(B) The addresses of the incorporators.

(C) The nature of the business or purposes to be conducted or promoted.

(D) None of the above answers is correct.

Facts for Question 2 (*)

Horizon Corp. is a Delaware corporation. It has two shareholders, namely Ernest and Bert. Each of them holds one share, and each of them is a director of the corporation. The corporation does not have any other directors. In former times, Ernest and Bert were good friends. Now, however, they fight all the time. They cannot agree on anything, and the corporation has not adopted any board resolutions for over a year. Which, if any, of the following statements is correct?

(A) If either Bert or Ernie requests the dissolution of the corporation, the Delaware Chancery Court may dissolve the corporation.

(B) The Delaware Chancery Court cannot dissolve the corporation.

(C) The Delaware Chancery Court can dissolve the corporation, but only if both Ernie and Bert request such a dissolution.

(D) None of the statements above is correct.

Facts for Question 3 (*)

Rebel Corp. is a Delaware corporation. It owns and operates an advertising agency. The corporation has four shareholders named Alexandra, Bella, Carl, and Dave. Rudy is the sole director of Rebel Corp. On January 5, 2014, after carefully investigating and analyzing all relevant facts, the board resolves to lease a new office for the corporation. The lease is twice as expensive as that for the old office, but the new office is much more centrally located and looks much more "upscale," which, in Rudy's opinion will make it much easier to attract new customers. The shareholders are furious. All of them are opposed to the board's decision. However, the next day, Rudy proceeds as planned and leases the new building while canceling the lease for the old office. Which of the following statements is most correct?

(A) Rudy has neither violated his duty of loyalty nor his duty of care.

(B) Rudy has violated his duty of care, but not his duty of loyalty.

(C) Rudy has violated his duty of loyalty, but not his duty of care.

(D) Rudy has violated both his duty of loyalty and his duty of care.

Facts for Question 4 (*)

Which of the following provisions cannot be included in the certificate of incorporation of a Delaware corporation without violating Delaware law.

(A) A provision limiting the duration of the corporation's existence to a specified date.

(B) A provision imposing personal liability for the debts of the corporation on its stockholders.

(C) A provision eliminating or limiting the liability of a director to the corporation or its stockholders for monetary damages for breach of the duty of loyalty.

(D) A provision requiring for certain corporate actions the vote of a supermajority of 90% of all shares entitled to vote on the matter.

Facts for Question 5 (**)

Hypo Corp. is a newly formed Delaware corporation. At its first board meeting on January 1, 2015, it issues ten par value shares with a par value of $10 per share at a price of $50 per share. The board does not adopt any resolution regarding the increase in the amount of capital. On June 1, 2015, the same corporation issues 10 no-par value shares at a price of $20 each. Again, the board makes no resolution regarding the increase in capital with respect to these shares. On August 8, 2015, the corporation's net assets amount to $10,000,000. The board decides, via resolution, that the capital shall be increased by $50,000. What is the capital of the corporation?

(A) $100.

(B) $300.

(C) $50,000.

(D) $50,300.

Facts for Question 6 (*)

Hypo Corp. is a Delaware corporation. Its capital is $10,000, its total liabilities amount to $5,000, and its total assets amount to $22,000. By how much can the board increase the corporation's capital without issuing additional shares?

(A) $8,000.

(B) $12,000.

(C) $17,000.

(D) None of the above.

Facts for Question 7 (*)

Under Delaware law, which, if any, of the following is true about the corporation's registered office.

    (A) It has to be located in Delaware.

    (B) It has to be located at the same place as the corporation's primary place of business.

    (C) It has to be located at the address of one of the corporation's incorporators.

    (D) None of the above statements is true.

Facts for Question 8 (*)

Which, if any, of the following is *not* true about the directors of a Delaware corporation.

    (A) The number of directors must be fixed in the certificate of incorporation.

    (B) A director may resign at any time.

    (C) Directors need not be stockholders unless so required by the certificate of incorporation or the bylaws.

    (D) All of the above statements are correct.

Facts for Question 9 (**)

Hypo Corp. owns $1,100,000 in cash and no other assets. It has liabilities in the amount of $100,000. Hypo Corp. has not made a profit for five years. It has ten shares outstanding. The corporation's legal capital equals $1,000,000. The board of Hypo Corp. wants Hypo Corp. to pay a dividend in the amount of $10,000 per share. Would this be legal?

    (A) Yes, Hypo Corp. can pay the dividend out of its surplus.

    (B) Yes, but only because of the nimble dividends rule.

    (C) Yes, despite the fact that the corporation does not have a surplus and despite the fact that the nimble dividends rule does not apply.

    (D) No, the payment of the dividend would not be legal.

Facts for Question 10 (*)

Gold Corp. is a closely-held Delaware corporation. George is the only director of Gold Corp. He was elected at an annual meeting that took place on January 11, 2014. In March 2014, it becomes obvious that George is completely incompetent and is mismanaging the corporation. The shareholders are eager to replace George with another director, but, under the corporation's bylaws, the next annual meeting will not be held until January 11, 2015. In addition, George vehemently refuses to call a special meeting. Can the shareholders remove George before then next annual meeting? Assume that the corporation's certificate of incorporation and bylaws do not mention special meetings.

    (A) Yes, because under Delaware law, a special meeting must be called if one quarter of the outstanding shares entitled to vote support such a request.

(B) Yes, the shareholders can remove George before the next annual meeting. They can do so by written consent.

(C) Yes. Directors cannot be removed without cause, but mismanagement constitutes cause for removal.

(D) No, it is not possible for the shareholders to remove George before the next annual meeting.

Facts for Question 11 (*)

Which, if any, of the following statements is correct?

(A) A majority of all closely held corporations in the United States are incorporated in Delaware.

(B) Under Delaware law, a short form merger in which the subsidiary corporation is the surviving corporation is called "consolidation."

(C) In the case of a short form merger under Delaware law, approval by the shareholders of the parent corporation is necessary only if the merger resolution amends the certificate of incorporation of the surviving corporation.

(D) None of the statements above is correct.

Facts for Question 12 (*)

Under the legal default (the rules that apply if neither the certificate of incorporation nor the bylaws provide for something else), which one of the following is *not* true.

(A) The board of directors may hold its meetings outside of Delaware.

(B) The board of directors has the authority to fix the compensation of directors.

(C) The board consists of one class of directors as opposed to being classified.

(D) One third of the total number of directors constitute a quorum for the transaction of business.

Facts for Question 13 (*)

Larry, Moe, and Bearle want to run a for-profit business together. It is important to them to avoid personal liability. Which of the following entity types does not confer protection against personal liability for all of its owners?

(A) The corporation.

(B) The limited liability company.

(C) The limited partnership.

(D) The statutory close corporation.

Facts for Question 14 (*)

Gold Corp. is a public corporation. It is incorporated in Delaware, all of its shareholders live in Illinois, and all of its board meetings take place in Texas, where all of the corporation's directors live. The corporation's primary place of business is located in Nevada. Which state law applies to the corporation's internal affairs?

(A) Delaware law.

(B) Illinois law.

(C) Texas law.

(D) Nevada law.

Facts for Question 15 (**)

Crouching Tiger Corp. is a Delaware corporation. Since its formation, Crouching Tiger Corp. has only issued ten shares. All of them are currently outstanding, and all of them are no-par value shares. All ten shares were issued on January 1, 2014, at a price of $1,000 per share in cash.

By January 15, 2014, the corporation's total assets have dwindled to $20,000, whereas the corporation's total liabilities amount to $21,000. Understandably, the board is quite concerned. That same day, the board, which had not addressed the issue in any prior resolution, holds a meeting attended by all of the corporation's directors. At the meeting, the directors unanimously adopt a resolution according to which "half of the consideration received for the shares issued on January 1, 2014, shall be capital." On January 18, 2014, the board has another meeting. At this point, the corporation's total assets amount to $7,000, whereas the corporation's total liabilities amount to $25,000. At the meeting on January 18, 2014, all board members are present and the board unanimously adopts a resolution according to which "$4,999 of the capital represented by the no-par value shares is hereby transferred to surplus, effective immediately." What is the corporation's capital immediately after the board meeting on January 18, 2014?

(A) $1.

(B) $5,000.

(C) $5,001.

(D) $10,000.

Facts for Question 16 (**)

Spring Corp., Summer Corp. and Fall Corp. are Delaware corporations. Each of these corporations has only one class of shares. On January 1, Spring Corp. purchases 51% of the common stock of Summer Corp. On January 2, Summer Corp. purchases 51% of the common stock of Fall Corp. On January 3, Fall Corp. purchases 1% of the common stock of Spring Corp. On May 1, Spring Corp.'s annual shareholder meeting takes place. Which of the following statements is correct?

(A) At Spring Corp.'s annual meeting, the shares held by Fall Corp. cannot be voted or counted for quorum purposes.

(B) At Spring Corp.'s annual meeting, the shares held by Fall Corp. cannot be voted, but they can be counted for quorum purposes.

   (C) At Spring Corp.'s annual meeting, the shares held by Fall Corp. can be voted, but they cannot be counted for quorum purposes.

   (D) At Spring Corp.'s annual meeting, the shares held by Fall Corp. can be voted, and they can also be counted for quorum purposes.

Facts for Question 17 (**)

Monday Corp, Tuesday Corp. and Wednesday Corp. are Delaware corporations. Each of these corporations has only one class of shares. On January 1, Monday Corp. purchases 51% of the common stock of Tuesday Corp. On January 2, Tuesday Corp. purchases 1% of the common stock of Wednesday Corp. On January 3, Wednesday Corp. purchases 51% of the common stock of Monday Corp. On May 1, Monday Corp.'s annual shareholder meeting takes place. Which of the following statements is correct?

   (A) At Monday Corp.'s annual meeting, the shares held by Wednesday Corp. cannot be voted or counted for quorum purposes.

   (B) At Monday Corp.'s annual meeting, the shares held by Wednesday Corp. cannot be voted, but they can be counted for quorum purposes.

   (C) At Monday Corp.'s annual meeting, the shares held by Wednesday Corp. can be voted, but they cannot be counted for quorum purposes.

   (D) At Monday Corp.'s annual meeting, the shares held by Wednesday Corp. can be voted, and they can also be counted for quorum purposes.

Facts for Question 18 (**)

Movie Corporation is a closely held corporation. Its certificate of incorporation provides that the corporation's directors are to be elected via cumulative voting. The certificate of incorporation also provides that the corporation's board shall have three directors. The corporation has issued ten shares since it was formed, and all of these ten shares are outstanding. Three of those ten shares are held by Julia, a well-known businesswoman who owns and runs a sole proprietorship with 200 employees. She wants to elect as many of her own employees as possible to the board of Movie Corporation. She assumes, correctly, that none of the other shareholders will vote for her employees. She does not know how many of the other shareholders will vote at the next annual shareholder meeting. Assuming that three directors will be elected at the next annual meeting of Movie Corporation, what is the minimum number of employees that Julia can expect to be able to elect as directors at the next annual shareholder meeting?

   (A) One.

   (B) Two.

   (C) Three.

   (D) None of the above.

Facts for Question 19 (**)

Vivian Corp. is a corporation with only one class of stock. On January 1, 2013, there are 100 shares of Vivian Corp. stock outstanding. Edward Corp. is a corporation with only one class of shares. On January 1, 2013, there are 100 shares of Edward Corp. stock outstanding.

On January 2, 2013, Lewis Corp. buys 60 shares of Vivian Corp. stock. Lewis Corp. is a corporation with only one class of stock. There are 100 shares of Lewis Corp. stock outstanding. On January 3, 2013, Vivian Corp. buys 5 shares of Edward Corp. stock. On January 4, 2013 Edward Corp. buys 40 shares of Lewis Corp. stock. According to its certificate of incorporation, Lewis Corp.'s board consists of a single director.

On March 6, 2013, Lewis Corp.'s annual shareholder meeting takes place. Among the candidates for the board are Morse, an employee of Edward Corp., and Kit. Edward Corp.'s board plans to vote all of its 40 Lewis Corp. shares for Morse, but another shareholder, Phil, who owns 30 Lewis Corp. shares, has already announced that he will vote his 30 Lewis Corp. shares for Kit. At the shareholder meeting, the shares held by Phil and those held by Edward Corp. are represented by proxy. No other shares are represented by proxy or present in person. Which of the following statements is most correct?

(A) Morse can expect to be elected to the board of Lewis Corp. at the shareholder meeting on March 6, 2013.

(B) Kit can expect to be elected to the board of Lewis Corp. at the shareholder meeting on March 6, 2013.

(C) Neither Morse nor Kit can expect to be elected to the board of Lewis Corp. at the shareholder meeting on March 6, 2013.

(D) None of the above.

Facts for Question 20 (**)

Thrifty Corp. is a Delaware corporation. Tim is Thrifty Corp.'s sole shareholder, and he is also Thrifty Corp.'s sole director and CEO. Tim always makes sure that all corporate formalities are scrupulously followed. Thrifty Corp.'s total assets amount to $100. Carla is a wealthy individual. On January 1, 2014, Thrifty Corp. and Carla enter into an agreement to open a restaurant together; under the agreement each of them shall get half of the profits. Unfortunately, the restaurant does not attract many patrons.

On January 5, 2014, Carla tells Tim: "Why don't you visit my old friend Rich tomorrow. He is very wealthy. Ask him for a loan to the restaurant in the amount of $100,000. I am sure he will fork over the money." Tim replies: "OK, I will try." On January 6, 2014, Tim—acting in the name of the "joint venture"—applies for a loan in the amount of $100,000 from Rich, a wealthy individual. Rich is somewhat hesitant, but Tim tells him: "Look, you know full well that Thrifty Corp. is part of the joint venture, and I, as CEO and sole owner of Thrifty Corp., assure you that Thrifty Corp. has more than enough money to pay you back at any time. Thrifty Corp. is swimming in cash." At the moment of this statement, Tim knows full well that Thrifty Corp.'s total assets only add up to $100. Because of Tim's false statement, Rich grants the loan to the "joint venture," and the loan agreement provides that the loan is to be paid back by December 31, 2014. When the loan comes due, the restaurant cannot pay it back. Rich wants to know whether he can hold Carla, Thrifty Corp., and/or Tim personally liable.

Which, if any, of the following statements is most correct?

(A) Rich can hold Carla liable, Rich can hold Thrifty Corp. liable, and Rich can hold Tim personally liable.

(B) Rich can hold Carla liable. Rich can hold Thrifty Corp. liable. By contrast, Rich will very probably not be able to hold Tim personally liable.

(C) Rich can hold Thrifty Corp. liable, but he can neither hold Carla nor Tim personally liable.

(D) None of the answers above is correct.

Facts for Question 21 (**)

Gold Corp. is a Delaware corporation that was formed in 1925. According to its certificate of incorporation, it has three directors. Furthermore, the certificate of incorporation grants the board the power to amend, adopt, or repeal bylaws. On January 16, 2014, the board unanimously adopts a bylaw according to which the board shall be classified and shall consist of three classes of directors. At the next shareholder meeting, the shareholders want to replace all three directors. Can they do so?

(A) Yes, because the bylaw classifying the board is void.

(B) Yes, the bylaw classifying the board is not void. However, the shareholder meeting can repeal the bylaw classifying the board with the effect that all directors are up for reelection.

(C) Yes, in case of a classified board, not all directors are up for reelection at each meeting. However, even in case of a classified board, the shareholders can remove directors at any time and without cause.

(D) No, the bylaw classifying the board is valid, and the shareholders cannot repeal a bylaw adopted by the board.

Facts for Question 22 (**)

Gold Corp. is a Delaware corporation. Its certificate of incorporation provides that the board shall have the power to adopt, amend, and repeal bylaws. At Gold Corp.'s 2014 annual shareholder meeting, 90% of the shares are present or represented by proxy, and 60% of the shares that are present or represented by proxy are voted in favor of a bylaw provision banning the use of poison pills by the corporation's board. Which of the following statements is most correct?

(A) The bylaw is void, but only because the shareholders no longer had the power to adopt bylaws.

(B) The bylaw is void, but only because it interferes with the board's power to manage or supervise the management of the corporation.

(C) The bylaw is void, but only because an insufficient number of shares were voted in favor of the bylaw.

(D) The bylaw is valid.

Facts for Question 23 (**)

Peter is the sole director of Gold Corp., a publicly traded Delaware corporation. In January 2014, Gold Corp. acquires 60% of the shares of Silver Corp., another publicly traded Delaware corporation in a cash-for-shares deal. This turns out to be a poor acquisition, as the value of the shares of Silver Corp. declines rapidly within the next few months.

Peter now considers two possible choices. First, Gold Corp. can sell the Silver Corp. shares, thereby realizing a loss which the corporation can deduct from its income and thereby lower its corporate income tax liability. For financial accounting purposes, this solution would make the corporation's net income for the year substantially lower because the net income would reflect the loss. Alternatively, Peter considers distributing the shares of Silver Corp. as a dividend to Gold Corp.'s own shareholders. This solution has the drawback that neither Gold Corp. nor Gold Corp.'s shareholders realize a loss for tax purposes. On the other hand, the advantage of this solution, as Peter sees it, would be that for financial accounting purposes, the loss resulting loss would be charged against surplus. Fearing that the stock market may react much more negatively to lower net income than to a mere reduction in surplus, Peter opts for the second solution and lets Gold Corp. distribute the shares of Silver Corp. as a dividend. Which of the following statements is most correct?

(A) Peter has violated his duty of care, and that is true even if the corporation's certificate of incorporation contains a so-called exculpation clause that eliminates the liability of directors to the fullest extent permitted by law.

(B) Peter has violated his duty of care, but only if the corporation's certificate of incorporation does not contain a so-called exculpation clause that eliminates the liability of directors to the fullest extent permitted by law.

(C) Peter has not violated his duty of care, but he has violated his duty of loyalty.

(D) Peter has neither violated his duty of care nor his duty of loyalty.

Facts for Question 24 (**)

Fredo is both the CEO and the chairman of the board of Family, Inc., a Delaware corporation. The other directors are Fredo's father, Vito, Fredo's older brother, Santino, and Fredo's younger brother, Michael.

None of the corporation's directors holds any shares in the corporation. Also, share ownership is widely dispersed. The corporation produces several successful movies. For the production of one of them, the corporation acquires a beautiful villa in Sicily, Italy. Following the filming of the movie, the relevant property is no longer used. Michael, after getting into some legal trouble in the United States, informs Fredo that he wants to buy the relevant property from the corporation in order to spend some time there. Michael offers to buy the property for $1,000,000.

Fredo thinks the relevant property is worth at most $700,000. The next day, Fredo brings the matter before the board. All directors are present except Michael, who is in Italy at the time. Fredo, who does not have any experience in real estate matters, tells the directors that Michael has offered to buy the property for one million dollars. He also points out that while he has not made any inquiries, he is sure that the property won't sell for more than seven hundred thousand dollars. Following Fredo's recommendation, the directors present at the board meeting unanimously resolve to sell the property to Michael. The next day, the corporation enters into a formal sales contract with Michael. Assume that the true market value of the property is $2,000,000.

Which, if any, of the following statements is correct?

(A) Fredo is liable to the corporation, but only because he has breached his duty of care.

(B) Fredo is liable to the corporation, but only because he has acted in bad faith.

(C) Fredo is not protected by the business judgment rule, and this would be true even if his belief that the property was worth $700,000 was based on careful investigation and analysis.

(D) None of the above statements is correct.

Facts for Question 25 (**)

Fredo is both the CEO and the chairman of the board of Family, Inc., a closely held Delaware Corporation with total assets in the amount of $20,000,000. The other directors are Fredo's father, Vito, Fredo's older brother, Santino, and Fredo's younger brother, Michael. On January 1, 2013, the corporation sells an old villa to Michael at a price of $1,000,000. The directors had unanimously approved the sale in the honest belief that this was the villa's true value. However, none of the directors made any effort to verify whether this assumption was correct, and the true market value of the villa was $10,000,000—a fact that any realtor could have told the corporation and that even the most cursory examination of real estate prices in the area would have revealed.

Luca, who has been a shareholder of the corporation for ten years, is outraged. He wants to sue the directors in the Delaware Chancery Court because he (Luca) thinks that they have violated "their duties." Which, if any, of the following statements is correct?

Which, if any, of the following statements is correct?

(A) The suit has to be brought as a derivative suit. However, demand will be excused on the grounds that it is futile.

(B) The suit has to be brought as a derivative suit, and demand will not be excused.

(C) The suit has to be brought as a direct suit (rather than as a derivative suit), but the demand requirement also applies to direct suits, and in this case, demand will not be excused.

(D) The suit has to be brought as a direct suit, and the demand requirement under Chancery Court Rule 23.1 does not apply to direct suits.

Facts for Question 26 (**)

Fredo is the sole director of Splurge Corp., a closely held Delaware Corporation with total assets in the amount of $20,000,000. In January 2014, he approves the sale of an old villa belonging to the corporation to Max for a price of $1,000,000. Fredo assumed the villa was worth $500,000, but never made any effort to verify this assumption. In fact, the true value of the villa was $10,000,000—a fact that any realtor could have told the corporation and that even the most cursory examination of real estate prices in the area would have revealed. The certificate of incorporation of Splurge Corp. contains an exculpation clause which "eliminates the liability of corporate directors for fiduciary duty violations to the fullest extent permitted by law." Which, if any, of the following statements is correct?

(A) The exculpation provision cannot protect Fredo from liability because he violated his duty of loyalty.

(B) The exculpation provision cannot protect Fredo from liability, but only because the sale of the property to Michael amounted to a distribution in violation of the legal capital rules.

(C) The exculpation provision cannot protect Fredo from liability because the certificate of incorporation may not limit or eliminate the liability of directors for fiduciary duty violations.

(D) In light of the exculpation provision, Fredo cannot be held liable with respect to the sale of the villa.

Facts for Question 27 (**)

Pizza Corp. is a Delaware corporation that owns and operates a restaurant offering a wide selection of pizza. It has ten shareholders, each of whom holds exactly one share. Paul, Maria, Christine, and Yael are among Pizza Corp.'s shareholders. Christine is the corporation's CEO. The corporation has two directors, namely Maria and Yael.

On January 1, 2000, when Paul sits in the restaurant enjoying a glass of wine, he is approached by a man he does not know. The man introduces himself as "Lee" and tells Paul: "I hear you are real savvy in the restaurant business. As it happens, my friends and I want to open up another pizza place about 2 miles from here, and we are looking for an investor. Would you care to become one of the shareholders of the corporation we want to form? You would have to invest $20,000." As they talk about it, Paul realizes that the offer is a great opportunity to make money. To be on the safe side, Paul calls Christine, tells her all about the offer and asks her if the corporation might be interested in investing. But Christine just says: "Are you kidding, we got our hands full running our own business," and hangs up. Thereupon, Paul accepts Lee's offer. In fact, Pizza Corp. would have had the necessary cash on hand to make use of the investment opportunity that Lee offered to Paul. Which, if any, of the following statements is true?

(A) Paul has violated his duty of loyalty, but not his duty of care.

(B) Paul has violated his duty of care, but not his duty of loyalty.

(C) Paul has not violated any fiduciary duties because he presented the opportunity to Christine and she declined it.

(D) Paul has not violated any fiduciary duties. The same would be true if he had not presented the opportunity to Christine before accepting it.

Facts for Question 28 (**)

Silver Corp. is a Delaware corporation. Its no-par value shares are currently traded at $1500 per share. Carl is Silver Corp.'s sole director. On January 1, 2013, Silver Corp. issues one no-par value share to George in exchange for a used car. Carl, who has carefully investigated the matter, believes in good faith that the car is worth $2000. Rudy is one of the shareholders of Silver Corp. He believes that the car is only worth $1000 at most. Assuming that Rudy is correct, which of the following statements is most correct?

(A) Carl has violated his duty of loyalty, and the transaction is voidable.

(B) Carl has violated his duty of loyalty, but the transaction is not voidable.

(C) Carl has not violated his duty of loyalty, but the transaction is voidable.

(D) Carl has not violated his duty of loyalty, and the transaction is not voidable either.

Facts for Question 29 (**)

Gold Corp. is a Delaware corporation. Its par value shares are currently traded at $200 per share, despite the fact that the par value is $600 per share.

Gold Corp. issues one par value share with a par value of $600 to Mark in exchange for an unsecured promissory note with a face value of $600. The board of Gold Corp. reasonably believes that the promissory note is actually worth $550. Does the transaction violate Delaware law? Which of the following statements is most correct?

(A) The transaction violates Delaware law, and this would be true even if the share issued to Mark had a par value of $400.

(B) The transaction violates Delaware law. By contrast, the transaction would be entirely legal if the share had a par value of $400.

(C) The transaction does not violate Delaware law, and the same would be true if the share had a par value of $400.

(D) The transaction does not violate Delaware law. By contrast, the transaction would be illegal if the share had a par value of $400.

Facts for Question 30 (**)

Gold Corp. is a Delaware corporation that was formed in 1925. Its certificate of incorporation explicitly grants the board the power to adopt, amend, or repeal bylaws. In 2015, the board decides that it would in the best interest of the corporation to have a classified board. Which, if any, of the following statements is *not* true?

(A) The board can be classified by amending the certificate of incorporation.

(B) Gold Corp.'s board can adopt a bylaw classifying the board.

(C) Gold Corp.'s shareholders can adopt a bylaw classifying the board.

(D) All of the statements above is true.

Facts for Question 31 (**)

Gold Corp. is a Delaware corporation. It owns and operates a car factory. That car factory accounts for 95% of the corporation's assets and 100% of the corporation's profits. The remaining assets take the form of a restaurant, which is not, however, profitable. In 2013, the board of Gold Corp. announces that it will lease the car factory to Silver Corp. because Gold Corp.'s own cars have become unfashionable, whereas Silver Corp. plans to use the factory to produce very profitable electric cars and is willing to compensate Gold Corp. handsomely for the use of Gold Corp.'s factory. Which of the following statements is most correct?

(A) The board's decision has to be approved by Gold Corp.'s shareholders, and the same would be true if the factory accounted for only 50% of Gold Corp.'s assets and if Gold Corp.'s remaining assets were profitable.

(B) The board's decision has to be approved by Gold Corp.'s shareholders. However, no such shareholder approval would be needed if the factory accounted for only 50% of Gold Corp.'s assets and if Gold Corp.'s remaining assets were profitable.

(C) The board's decision does not have to be approved by Gold Corp.'s shareholders, and the same would be true if Gold Corp. had sold—rather than leased—the factory to Silver Corp.

(D) The board's decision does not have to be approved by Gold Corp.'s shareholders. However, shareholder approval would be needed if Gold Corp. had sold—rather than leased—the factory to Silver Corp.

Facts for Question 32 (**)

Miriam Corp. is a publicly traded Delaware corporation. According to its certificate of incorporation, its board has five directors. As of January 1, 2000, these five directors are Tim, Tom, Mary, Larry, and Clarinda. Tom, Mary, and Larry are Tim's children. Tim does not have any ties to Clarinda.

On February 1, 2000, Tim buys a parcel of real estate from Miriam Corp. at a price of $1,000,000. At the time of the transaction, the market value of the property is $1,200,000.

Before the relevant documents are signed, the transaction is approved by the board of Miriam Corp. At the relevant board meeting, which takes place on February 1, 2000, all directors are present, and four of them approve the transaction, with only Clarinda voting against it.

On March 1, 2000, the annual shareholder meeting of Miriam Corp. takes place. Tim and Tom are reelected to the board. By contrast, Mary, Larry, and Clarinda are not reelected. In their stead Matt, Joanne, and Justin are elected to the board. None of the three new directors has any ties to Tim, Tom, Marry, Larry, or Clarinda.

Jill is a longtime shareholder of Miriam Corp. On April 1, 2000, Jill brings a derivative suit with the aim of making Tim pay damages to the corporation.

Jill did not make any demand on the board of Miriam Corp. before filing her derivative suit. Jill owns 67% of the outstanding shares of Miriam Corp. Which, if any, of the following statements is correct?

    (A)   Demand is excused. However, the derivative suit will be dismissed because Jill cannot fairly and adequately represent the interests of the other shareholders.

    (B)   The derivative suit will be dismissed because demand is not excused. By contrast, there is no reason to believe that Jill cannot fairly and adequately represent the interest of the other shareholders.

    (C)   The derivative suit will be dismissed both because demand was not excused and because Jill cannot fairly and adequately represent the interest of the other shareholders.

    (D)   Jill's derivative suit will not be dismissed.

Facts for Question 33 (**)

Miriam Corp. is a publicly traded Delaware corporation. According to its certificate of incorporation, its board has five directors. As of January 1, 2000, these five directors are Tim, Tom, Mary, Larry, and Clarinda. Tom, Mary, and Larry are Tim's children. Tim does not have any ties to Clarinda.

On February 1, 2000, Tim buys a parcel of real estate from Miriam Corp. at a price of $1,000,000. At the time of the transaction, the market value of the property is $1,200,000.

Before the relevant documents are signed, the transaction is approved by the board of Miriam Corp. At the relevant board meeting, which takes place on February 1, 2000, all directors are present, and four of them approve the transaction, with only Clarinda voting against it.

Jill is a longtime shareholder of Miriam Corp. Since 1995, she has been the owner of 67% of the outstanding shares of Miriam Corp. On March 1, 2000,

Jill presents the board of Miriam Corp. with a written demand to sue Tim for damages. However, the board, on March 15, 2000, decides via a unanimous resolution not to bring suit against Tim. On April 1, 2000, Jill brings a derivative suit with the aim of making Tim pay damages to the corporation. Which, if any, of the following statements is true?

  (A) Jill's derivative suit will be dismissed unless she can show that the board of Miriam Corp. acted in bad faith or without being reasonably informed when it decided not to bring suit against Tim.

  (B) Jill's derivative suit will be dismissed, but only if the board of Miriam Corp. can show that it acted in good faith and in a reasonably informed fashion when it decided not to bring suit against Tim.

  (C) Jill's derivative suit will not be dismissed because the directors of Miriam Corp. were not disinterested when they decided not to bring suit against Tim.

  (D) Jill's derivative suit will not be dismissed because she has made a prior demand on the corporation. This outcome would be the same even if the directors of Miriam Corp. did not have a conflict of interest.

Facts for Question 34 (**)

Miriam Corp. is a publicly traded Delaware corporation. According to its certificate of incorporation, its board has five directors. As of January 1, 2000, these five directors are Tim, Tom, Mary, Larry, and Clarinda. Tom, Mary, and Larry are Tim's children. Tim does not have any ties to Clarinda.

On February 1, 2000, Tim buys a parcel of real estate from Miriam Corp. at a price of $1,000,000. At the time of the transaction, the market value of the property is $1,200,000.

Before the relevant documents are signed, the transaction is approved by the board of Miriam Corp. At the relevant board meeting, which takes place on February 1, 2000, all directors are present, and four of them approve the transaction, with only Clarinda voting against it.

Jill is a longtime shareholder of Miriam Corp. Since 1995, she has been the owner of 67% of the outstanding shares of Miriam Corp. On March 1, 2000, Jill files a derivate suit in the Delaware Chancery Court. The corporation asks the Court to dismiss the suit because Jill never made a demand upon the corporation, but the Court deems the suit to be admissible.

On May 1, 2000, the annual shareholder meeting of Miriam Corp. takes place. The shareholders, outraged at the behavior of the board, elect five new directors: Jack, Joe, Jim, James, and Mike. On June 1, 2000, the new board creates a "litigation committee" consisting of Jack, Joe, and Jim. On July 1, 2000, the litigation committee is entrusted with the task of evaluating whether the dismissal of the derivative suit is in the best interest of the corporation. The litigation committee unanimously adopts a resolution according to which the derivative suit is not in the best interest of the corporation and should be dismissed.

Miriam Corp. submits this resolution to the Chancery Court and asks the Court to dismiss Jill's suit.

Which, if any, of the following statements is correct?

(A) If the Chancery Court, exercising its own business judgment, deems the dismissal of the suit to be in the best interest of Miriam Corp., it will dismiss the suit unless Jill can show that the litigation committee acted in the presence of a conflict of interest, in bad faith, or without being reasonably informed.

(B) If the Court, exercising its own business judgment, deems the dismissal of the suit to be in the best interest of Miriam Corp., it will dismiss the suit, but only if the corporation can show that the litigation committee was reasonably informed and disinterested and acted in good faith.

(C) The Court will automatically dismiss the suit unless Jill can show that the litigation committee acted in the presence of a conflict of interest, in bad faith, or without being reasonably informed.

(D) The Court will automatically dismiss the suit, but only if the corporation can show that the litigation committee was reasonably informed and disinterested and acted in good faith.

Facts for Question 35 (**)

Heist Corp. is a privately held corporation with annual revenues of about $50,000,000. Since 1995, the board of Heist Corp. has had three members, namely Steven, Alice, and Wally.

One of the corporation's accountants is Catherine. Unfortunately, Catherine, who is paid a salary of $70,000 a year, has long had a gambling problem and, starting in 1996, has managed to steal large amounts of money— about $2,000,000 a year—from the corporation to finance her ever-increasing gambling losses.

Steven, Alice, and Wally have always been unaware of the fact that Catherine is stealing money from the corporation. However, on December 1, 1998, Steven comes across a newspaper article on Las Vegas featuring a picture of Catherine and describing her as "a daring roulette player, often betting hundreds of thousands of dollars in a single night." Steven immediately recognizes Catherine in the picture. He is mildly curious as to how Catherine is financing her hobby because he knows that Catherine is from a family of modest means and has had to hold various jobs to finance her college education. However, Steven does not follow up because he thinks that perhaps Catherine has "won the lottery or something," even though, shortly before, another accountant, Bill, has alerted Steven to the fact that some of the numbers for which Catherine was responsible in the accounting department "seem to be wrong in a really big way."

From 1999 to 2000, Catherine manages to steal another $4,000,000 from the corporation. At the beginning of 2001, her actions are discovered. Unfortunately for the corporation, Catherine has gambled away all of the money she has stolen, and so none of the money can be recovered. The corporation's certificate of incorporation does not include a liability waiver for fiduciary duty violations.

Does Steven risk being held personally liable?

(A) Yes, unless the corporation had in place an internal monitoring system designed to detect wrongdoing on the part of the employees.

(B) Yes because he acted in bad faith.

(C) No because directors are entitled to rely on the reports prepared by the corporation's employees.

(D) None of the three statements above (A, B, C) is correct.

Facts for Question 36 (**)

Big Corp. and Small Corp. are Delaware corporations. Each of them has only one class of shares. Big Corp. holds 92% of the shares issued by Small Corp. In January 2014, both corporations merge, with Small Corp. being the surviving corporation. Which of the following statements is correct?

(A) The merger does not have to be approved by Big Corp.'s shareholders, and that is true regardless of whether the merger is undertaken as a long-form merger or a short-form merger.

(B) If the merger is undertaken as a short form merger, then it does not have to be approved by Big Corp.'s shareholders. By contrast, if the merger is undertaken as a long-form merger, then it does have to be approved by Big Corp.'s shareholders.

(C) If the merger is undertaken as a long-form merger, then it does not have to be approved by Big Corp.'s shareholders. By contrast, if the merger is undertaken as a short-form merger, then it does have to be approved by Big Corp.'s shareholders.

(D) The merger has to be approved by Big Corp.'s shareholders regardless of whether it is a long-form merger or a short-form merger.

Facts for Question 37 (**)

Gold Corp. and Silver Corp. are both Delaware corporations. Silver Corp. has only one class of stock. Gold Corp. owns 92% of the shares of Silver Corp. The board of Gold Corp. wants to merge Gold Corp. with Silver Corp., and Gold Corp. is to be the surviving corporation. Will it be possible to merge both corporations without allowing the minority shareholders of Silver Corp. to vote on the merger?

(A) No, because a merger must always be approved by a majority of the shareholders in both corporations.

(B) No, because a merger must always be approved by the shareholders of the non-surviving corporation.

(C) Yes, and the same would be true if Silver Corp. were the surviving corporation.

(D) Yes, but if Silver Corp. were the surviving corporation, then the approval of the minority shareholders of Silver Corp. would be needed for the merger.

Facts for Question 38 (**)

Gold Corp. and Silver Corp. are publicly traded Delaware corporations. Each of these corporations has only one class of shares, and these shares are listed on the New York Stock Exchange. In 2014, both corporations merge in a so-called long form merger under DGCL § 251, with Gold Corp. being the surviving corporation.

George is a shareholder of Gold Corp. He has voted against the merger, and he had sent a letter to the board of Gold. Corp. before the merger vote, demanding appraisal. Under the merger agreement, George will receive $1000 in cash for every Gold share he held. By contrast, each Silver Corp. shareholder will receive 2 shares in the surviving corporation for each Silver Corp. share. 12 days after the meeting, George sent a written letter to the corporation demanding appraisal. The corporation declined.

George, who has held his Gold Corp. shares since 2012, now wants to know if he is entitled to appraisal. Which of the following statements is most correct?

(A) George is not entitled to appraisal. Appraisal is not available when the shares of the corporations involved in the merger are listed on a national securities exchange.

(B) George is not entitled to appraisal. Appraisal is not available when a shareholder receives cash for his shares.

(C) George is entitled to appraisal, and this would be true even if he had not notified the board of Gold Corp. of his desire to seek appraisal before the merger vote.

(D) George is entitled to appraisal, but this would not be true if he had failed to notify the board of Gold Corp. of his desire to seek appraisal.

Facts for Question 39 (**)

Delicious Corp. owns and operates a bakery. The corporation has three shareholders, namely Tina, Alexandra, and John, each of whom owns exactly one share. Since the corporation was formed in 2005, each of the three shareholders has continuously occupied a place on the board, and each of them has continuously worked at the bakery as an employee in exchange for a steady salary. The corporation has never paid any dividends.

In late 2015, Alexandra and John have a fallout over personal matters, and after that, the two do not get along anymore. Subsequently, Alexandra persuades Tina that it is in the best interest of the corporation if John is not reelected to the board and if his employment with the corporation is also terminated. Accordingly, at the next annual shareholder meeting, Tina and Alexandra use their votes to elect Alexandra, Tina, and their friend George to the board. The next day, the corporation fires John from his job at the bakery. Which of the following statements is most correct?

(A) Under Delaware's oppression statute, a court can dissolve a closely held corporation if those in control oppress the minority shareholders.

(B) Unlike various other states, Delaware has not adopted an oppression statute. However, under Delaware law, closely held corporations are governed by so-called "partnership-style" fiduciary duties. As a result, the corporation has to treat all shareholders equally, unless it can show a legitimate reason for disparate treatment. Given that John's personal fallout with Alexandra is no legitimate reason for disparate treatment, John's termination and the failure to reelect him as a director were illegal.

(C) Delaware has adopted both an oppression statute and partnership-style fiduciary duties for closely held corporations.

(D) Delaware has adopted neither an oppression statute nor partnership-style fiduciary duties for closely held corporations.

Facts for Question 40 (**)

George owns 90% of the shares of Truffles Corp., a Delaware corporation. On January 1, 2014, the shares of Truffles Corp. are listed at $100 per share. That same day, George sells his entire stake for $200 per share to Alexandra in a private transaction. Alexandra hopes to install new management and reduce the workforce of the company by 50%. Nyusha is a minority shareholder in Truffles Corp. She wants to know if she can somehow, directly or indirectly, participate in the premium that George received for his shares. Which of the following statements is most correct?

(A) Under the so-called corporate opportunity doctrine, George has to pass the control premium ($100 per share) on to the corporation. Therefore, Nyusha profits indirectly.

(B) Under the Williams Act, Alexandra has a duty to acquire shares pro rata from all shareholders willing to sell, and at the same price. Therefore, Nyusha can sell her shares to Alexandra at the same price that George did.

(C) Under the so-called looting doctrine, Nyusha can demand damages from George.

(D) George does not have to share the consideration that he received with anyone, and he does not owe damages either. Moreover, Alexandra has no duty to purchase shares from Nyusha.

Facts for Question 41 (*)

Which, if any, of the following statements is correct?

(A) In case of a long-form merger under Delaware law, the minority shareholders must be given the option of receiving shares in the surviving corporation, unless they receive, as consideration for their shares, shares in another publicly traded corporation or cash in lieu of fractional shares.

(B) "Scorched earth," "Pac-Man," "greenmail," and "black tower" are all names that are frequently used to refer to certain antitakeover defenses.

(C) A board can be classified into up to five classes of directors.

(D) None of the statements above is correct.

Facts for Question 42 (**)

Which, if any, of the following four statements (A, B, C, D) is correct?

(A) A corporate board cannot have more than 14 directors.

(B) A corporation cannot ban the use of poison pills in its certificate of incorporation.

(C) Under Delaware law, directors can never take into account the interests of stakeholders such as workers in making their decision.

(D) None of the three statements above (A, B, C) is correct.

Facts for Question 43 (**)

Bride Corp., Groom Corp., and Hostile Corp. are publicly traded Delaware corporations. Bride Corp. owns and operates an online travel agency. Groom Corp. owns and operates a hotel chain. Both corporations plan to merge because they hope to create substantial synergies by combining their two businesses. They sign a merger agreement, which contains a so-called "fiduciary out." Before the merger agreement was announced, the shares of Bride Corp. were traded at $50 per share. Under the merger agreement, each Bride Corp. shareholder will receive one share in the surviving corporation for each old Bride Corp. share, and the shares in the surviving corporation are thought to be worth about $60 per share. Before the merger, Bride Corp. does not have a controlling shareholder. However, after the merger, the surviving corporation will be controlled by Linus, who is currently the controlling shareholder of Groom Corp.

The day after the merger agreement is signed, Hostile Corp. announces that it will launch a hostile tender offer for 90% of Bride Corp.'s shares at a price of $100 per share. Concerned that this bid will derail the merger, the board of Bride Corp. adopts a poison pill that is triggered if any hostile bidder acquires 20% or more of Bride Corp.'s shares. Which standard of scrutiny will the court apply to the board's decision to adopt the poison pill?

(A) The so-called business judgment rule.

(B) The so-called Unocal standard.

(C) The so-called Weinberger Standard.

(D) The so-called Revlon standard.

Facts for Question 44 (**)

Target Corp. is a publicly traded corporation that does not have a controlling shareholder. On January 1, 2013, Hostile Corp. announces that it will launch a tender offer in order to acquire a controlling stake in Target Corp.

The board of Target Corp. meets on January 2, 2013. After careful consideration of the facts, the directors of Target Corp. come to the conclusion that "our days as an independent corporation are numbered" and that "whoever acquires Target Corp. will sell of its various divisions piece by piece." However, because the board is unhappy with the terms of Hostile Corp.'s planned tender offer, the board of Target Corp. starts looking around for another potential acquirer and finally decides to pursue a merger with Friendly Corp., another publicly traded corporation. Friendly Corp. is currently controlled by Solon, a wealthy investor who owns 96% of the stock of Friendly Corp. If the merger with Friendly Corp. takes place as planned, Solon will own 57% of the shares of the surviving corporation. Target Corp.'s board adopts a poison pill to ensure Hostile Corp. cannot derail the merger with Friendly Corp. In case of a lawsuit, which standard of scrutiny will a court likely apply to the decision of Target Corp.'s board to adopt the poison pill? Which, if any, of the following statements is correct?

(A) The so-called business judgment rule.

(B) The so-called Time Warner standard.

(C) The so-called Revlon standard.

(D) The so-called Weinberger standard.

Facts for Question 45 (***)

Target Corp. and Bidder Corp. are publicly traded corporations. The certificate of incorporation of Target Corp. contains a provision that prohibits Target Corp.'s board from taking defensive measures against takeovers. On January 1, 2014, the CEO of Bidder Corp. announces that he will soon launch a tender offer to acquire 90% of Target Corp.'s shares. He notes that the tender offer price will be around $100 per share. Although Target Corp.'s shares have lately been trading at $40, the directors of Target Corp. believe that the tender offer price suggested by Bidder Corp.'s CEO is much too low. Therefore, after careful investigation and analysis of all pertinent facts, the board of Target Corp. unanimously adopts a flip-in poison pill. Which of the following statements is correct?

(A) The adoption of the poison pill is void, but only because it violates Target Corp.'s charter.

(B) The adoption of the poison pill is void, and this would be true even if Target Corp.'s charter did not contain a ban on antitakeover measures.

(C) The adoption of the poison pill is legal, but only because the charter provision banning antitakeover measures is void.

(D) The adoption of the poison pill is legal despite the fact that the charter provision banning antitakeover measures is legal.

Facts for Question 46 (***)

Operator Corp. is a Delaware corporation. Mark is Operator Corp.'s sole shareholder, and he is also Operator Corp.'s sole director and CEO. Mark always makes sure that all corporate formalities are scrupulously followed. Operator Corp.'s total assets amount to $10, a fact that Mark is well aware of. Alicia is a wealthy individual.

On January 1, 2013, Alicia and Mark—the latter acting in his capacity as Operator Corp.'s CEO—both sign a written agreement entitled "Joint Venture Agreement." That agreement provides:

"Operator Corp. and Alicia hereby start a joint venture. The purpose of the joint venture is to own and operate a restaurant. Alicia and Operator Corp. will each receive 50% of the profits that the joint venture makes."

Assume that the applicable state law has no special legal rules for "joint ventures."

On January 2, 2013, Alicia orders two restaurant tables at a total price of $400 from Gregory, a supplier. She makes it clear that she is acting for "the joint venture between Alicia and Operator Corp.," and promises that Gregory will be paid by January 7, 2013. The next day, Gregory delivers the tables. When he demands payment two weeks later, the "joint venture" has no assets left. George wants to know who is liable to him for the $400.

(A) George can hold Alicia liable, George can hold Operator Corp. liable, George can hold the "joint venture" liable, and he (George) can very probably hold Mark liable.

(B) George can hold Alicia liable. He (George) can hold Operator Corp. liable. George can hold the "joint venture" liable. By contrast, George will very probably not be able to hold Mark personally liable.

(C) George can hold Operator Corp. liable, and he (George) can hold the "joint venture" liable. By contrast, neither Alicia nor Mark can be held personally liable by George.

(D) George can very probably hold Mark liable. George can hold Operator Corp. liable. George can hold the "joint venture" liable. By contrast, George cannot hold Alicia personally liable.

Facts for Question 47 (***)

Peter is the sole director of Gold Corp., a publicly traded Delaware corporation. He also owns 1% of the shares of Gold Corp. In January 2014, Peter, acting in his capacity as Gold Corp.'s sole director, hires his sister Pamela to do consulting work for the corporation. Pamela is paid $200,000 for her services. In fact, however, her work is largely useless, and Peter knew this in advance; he hired her solely because she is his favorite sister.

When the shareholders find out about the contract between Pamela and the corporation, they are furious. John has been a shareholder of the corporation for ten years. He brings a derivative suit against Peter asserting a breach of the duty of loyalty, and the Delaware Chancery Court ends up deciding that Peter has to pay damages to the corporation in the amount of $200,000. Moreover, at the next annual meeting, Peter is not reelected; instead, the shareholders elect Tom as Gold Corp.'s next director. Tom believes it is bad for the corporation's reputation if Peter is "left out in the cold." Also,

Tom points out that the corporation's articles of incorporation contain a provision according to which "all directors shall be fully indemnified against expenses and judgments, regardless of whether they acted in good faith."

Therefore, Tom decides that the corporation will indemnify Peter both with respect to the judgment ($200,000) and regarding the legal expenses that Peter has incurred ($40,000). Which of the following statements is most correct?

(A) Tom's decision is legal, but only if the corporation's articles of incorporation contain a so-called exculpation clause.

(B) Tom's decision is legal, and this is true regardless of whether the corporation's articles of incorporation contain an exculpation clause.

(C) Tom's decision is illegal, because it amounts to an illegal dividend.

(D) Tom's decision is illegal, and that is true despite the fact that the payment that Tom wants the corporation to make does not constitute a dividend.

Facts for Question 48 (***)

Angel Corp. is a publicly traded corporation. Angel Corp. has only one class of stock. Its board is not classified. Cordelia owns 91% of the shares of Angel Corp. On January 1, 2000, Michelle calls Cordelia and tells her that she wants to buy Cordelia's stake in Angel Corp. at a "fat premium" over the listing price. In fact, the premium alone is to amount to $100,000,000. Michelle truthfully tells Cordelia that once she (Michelle) has bought the shares held by Cordelia, she (Michelle) wants to merge Angel Corp. unto Demon Corp., a corporation that is wholly owned by Michelle. Michelle plans to undertake the merger in such a way as to cash out the minority shareholders of Angel Corp. Cordelia wants to accept Michelle's offer. Which, if any, of the following four statements is true?

(A) Cordelia will be able to keep the entire premium to herself. However, if Michelle wants to merge Angel Corp. unto Demon Corp. within three years after acquiring Cordelia's stake, she will need the approval of the board of Angel Corp. that is in place at the time of the transaction with Cordelia. In exchange for giving its approval, the board has to try to get something in return from Michelle and that something will benefit all the shareholders of Angel Corp., including the minority shareholders.

(B) Cordelia will be able to keep the entire premium to herself. Moreover, Michelle will not need the approval of the board of Angel Corp. that is in place at the time of the transaction with Cordelia in order to carry out the merger. That would be true even if the stake acquired from Cordelia only comprised 89% of Angel Corp.'s shares.

(C) Cordelia will not be able to keep the entire premium to herself because the planned merger with Angel Corp. falls under the so-called looting doctrine.

(D) Cordelia will be able to keep the entire premium to herself. However, this would not be true if the stake comprised less than 90% of Angel Corp.'s stock because, in that case, Michelle would have to launch a tender offer before being able to carry out the planned merger.

Facts for Question 49 (***)

Which, if any, of the following statements is true?

(A) In a long form merger, the merger agreement may amend the certificate of incorporation of the surviving corporation, but only to the extent that the merger complies with the general rules on charter amendments.

(B) In a short form merger, the certificate of incorporation of the surviving corporation can sometimes be amended without complying with the general rules on charter amendments, but in that case, the merger must always be approved by the shareholders of the surviving corporation.

(C) The par value of shares cannot be changed without the unanimous consent of the par value shareholders.

(D) None of the three statements above is true.

Facts for Question 50 (***)

Inertia Corp. is a publicly traded corporation. Its shares are listed on the New York Stock Exchange. Inertia Corp. has three divisions, all of which are organized as wholly owned subsidiary corporations of Inertia Corp. These subsidiary corporations concentrate on three completely different fields, namely waste disposal, space-exploration related technology ("rocket science"), and diapers.

Ann is a shareholder of Inertia Corp. Since January 1, 1995, she has held 100 Inertia Corp. shares. After she bought the shares in 1995 for a total price of $20,000, their value reached its lowest point on January 2, 1997, when their total value was $5,000. Over the following years, the shares' total value was always between $5,000 and $6,000. Ann is outraged at this development of the value of her shares.

In 1997, Ann decides to get active. That same year, she asks the corporation to include into its proxy materials a shareholder proposal. The proposal asks for a shareholder resolution recommending that the board "break up" the corporation by selling its many different divisions. However, the board wants to exclude the proposal from the corporation's proxy materials. Which of the following statements, if any, is true?

(A) In its current form, the proposal can be excluded on the ground that it violates state law and on the ground that it interferes with management functions.

(B) In its current form, the proposal can be excluded on the ground that it violates state law. It cannot, however, be excluded on the ground that it interferes with management functions.

(C) In its current form, the proposal cannot be excluded on the ground that it violates state law. Nor can it be excluded on the ground that it interferes with management functions.

(D) None of the three statements above (A, B, C) is true.

CHAPTER 4
LIMITED LIABILITY COMPANIES

Facts for Question 1 (*)

John, Jay, Alexandra, and Sylvia form a limited liability company under the law of the state of Delaware. The limited liability company agreement is silent on who manages the company. Which of the following answers is most correct?

(A) The company will be managed by its owners, unless the limited liability company agreement vests the power to manage the company in managers.

(B) The company will be managed by its owners, and this rule is mandatory.

(C) The company will be managed by one or more managers, unless the limited liability company agreement vests the power to manage the company in the company's owners.

(D) The company will be managed by one or more managers, and this rule is mandatory.

Facts for Question 2 (*)

John, Jay, Alexandra, and Sylvia have formed a member-managed limited liability company under the law of the state of Delaware. Jay delegates his "right and power to manage the limited liability company" to his employee Frank. The agreement states that this delegation is "irrevocable." Three weeks later, Jay declares that he "revokes the delegation." Which of the following statements is correct?

(A) The power to manage an LLC cannot be delegated.

(B) The power to manage an LLC can be delegated, but not in an irrevocable fashion.

(C) Jay has delegated his power to manage the LLC, and that delegation is irrevocable.

(D) Jay stopped being a member of the LLC when he delegated his power to manage the LLC.

Facts for Question 3 (*)

John, Jay, Alexandra, and Sylvia have formed a member-managed limited liability company under law of the state of Delaware. Under the LLC agreement, the sole purpose of the LLC is to run a store for fishing equipment located on the shore of Lake Peaceful. Unfortunately, Lake Peaceful, once a popular tourist destination permanently turns into a desert as a result of global warming, reducing the demand for fishing equipment to zero. Soon thereafter, on January 1, 2015, John dies of a heart attack. On January 5, 2015, Alexandra and Sylvia catch Jay as he tries to steal the remaining cash from the LLC's safe. On the spot, they tell him that he, Jay, is expelled from the LLC. The LLC agreement is silent on whether a member can be expelled from the LLC. Which of the following statements is correct?

(A) The LLC was dissolved when John died.

(B) The LLC was not dissolved when John died; but Jay ceased to be a member of the LLC when Alexandra and Sylvia expelled him.

(C) The LLC was not dissolved when John died; but it was dissolved when the lake dried up.

(D) The Delaware Court of Chancery can dissolve the LLC at the request of a member, and that would be true even if Jay had not tried to steal from the LLC.

Facts for Question 4 (*)

Ambitious Corp. is a Delaware corporation. It wants to form a Delaware LLC in which Ambitious Corp. is the sole member. Which of the following answers is correct?

(A) A Delaware LLC must have more than one member.

(B) A Delaware LLC can have a single member, but that member has to be a natural person.

(C) A Delaware LLC can have a single member, and that member can be a corporation, as long as it is a Delaware corporation.

(D) A Delaware LLC can have a single member, and that member can be a corporation. The corporation does not have to be a Delaware corporation.

Facts for Question 5 (*)

Tim, Tom, Mary, and Larry are members of a Delaware limited liability company. The going concern value of the LLC's business is $400,000. The liquidation value is $100,000. Tim decides that it's time to "cash in." When all four members meet on January 1, 2015, Tim declares that he "withdraws" from the corporation, and demands to be paid $100,000 in exchange for his membership? Which, if any, of the following statements is correct?

(A) Tim's withdrawal has dissolved the LLC. The LLC's business will be wound up, which in this case means it will be sold as a going concern. If the members manage to sell the business for $400,000, then Tim will get his share in the amount of $100,000.

(B) Tim's withdrawal has not dissolved the LLC. Moreover, the LLC now has an obligation to pay Tim the value of his membership. That means that Tim can demand to be paid $100,000.

(C) Tim does not have the power or the right to resign from the LLC.

(D) None of the answers above is correct.

Facts for Question 6 (*)

Tim, Tom, Mary, and Larry are members of a manager-managed limited liability company formed under Delaware law. The LLC's manager is George. On January 1, 2014, George, acting on behalf of the LLC, sells a car belonging to the LLC to his brother Frank at a price of $12,000. Tim finds out about this transaction, and several experts assure him that the fair market value of the car was at least $15,000. Therefore, Tim immediately files a derivative suit with the aim of making George pay damages to the LLC. In his complaint, he points out both the fact that George is Frank's brother and the evidence suggesting that the price was likely well below market. Which, if any, of the following answers is correct?

(A) The suit is inadmissible because Delaware LLC law does not allow for derivative suits.

(B) The suit is inadmissible. Delaware LLC law allows for derivative suits, but requires the plaintiff to make a prior demand on the LLC, and George has not satisfied the demand requirement.

(C) The suit is admissible. Delaware LLC law allows for derivative suits, and Delaware LLC law does not impose any demand requirement.

(D) None of the choices above is correct.

Facts for Question 7 (*)

Tim and Peter want to form an LLC under Delaware law. Their attorney has drafted an LLC agreement for the company. Now Tim and Peter want to know what has to be included in the LLC's certificate of formation. Which of the following statements, if any, is correct?

(A) The certificate of formation must include the LLC's name, the address of the LLC's registered office, and the name and address of its registered agent. However, the certificate of formation may not include any other provisions.

(B) The certificate of formation is identical to the LLC agreement. Therefore, by definition, every provision contained in the LLC agreement is also contained in the certificate of formation.

(C) The LLC agreement is not identical to the certificate of formation, but a provision in the LLC agreement is only enforceable if it is also contained in the certificate of formation.

(D) None of the choices above is correct.

Facts for Question 8 (*)

Tim and Peter want to form an LLC under Delaware law. Under the LLC agreement, each member is to make a contribution to the LLC. Which, if any, of the following types of contribution cannot be provided for in an LLC agreement?

(A) Services rendered.

(B) Promissory notes.

(C) Cash.

(D) All the different types of contributions listed above can be provided for in an LLC agreement.

Facts for Question 9 (*)

George and Peter have formed a Delaware LLC. Under the LLC agreement, George must contribute $1000 to the LLC, whereas Peter must contribute $2000. So far, George and Peter have each contributed $1000, meaning that Peter still owes part of his promised contribution. The agreement further provides that when decisions are to be made by the LLC's members, George will have one vote and Peter will have two votes. The LLC agreement does not mention profits. In 2014, the LLC makes a profit in the amount of $3000. How will this profit be allocated among the LLC's members?

(A) $1500 will be allocated to Peter, and $1500 will be allocated to George, because the default is that each member receives the same share of the profits.

(B) $1500 will be allocated to Peter, and $1500 will be allocated to George, because, so far, each of them has contributed $1000 to the LLC.

(C) $2000 will be allocated to Peter, and $1000 will be allocated to George, because under the legal default, the value of the promised contribution determines a member's shares of the profit.

(D) $2000 will be allocated to Peter, and $1000 will be allocated to George, because under the legal default, a member's voting rights determine his share of the profit.

Facts for Question 10 (*)

In 2013, George and Peter formed a Delaware LLC. Under the LLC agreement, George must contribute $1000 to the LLC, whereas Peter must contribute $2000. George immediately pays his promised contribution, whereas Peter decides to wait until 2014 to pay. The LLC agreement provides that if a member does not make all of his promised contribution by December 31, 2014, that member's interest in the LLC shall automatically be eliminated. In 2014, Peter loses his job and goes through a bitter divorce. As a result, he does not have the necessary cash to pay any of his contribution. He asks George for financial help, but George refuses to help. By December 31, 2014, Peter still has not paid any of his promised contribution. As of January 1, 2015, which, if any, of the following statements is correct?

(A) Peter's interest in the LLC has not been reduced or eliminated because the provision in the LLC agreement that calls for the elimination of a member's interest is void.

(B) Peter's interest in the LLC has not been eliminated, but it has been reduced.

(C) Peter's interest in the LLC has been eliminated.

(D) None of the statements above is correct.

Facts for Question 11 (*)

George and Peter want to form a manager-managed Delaware LLC. They want to eliminate, to the fullest extent possible, any liability for the violation of fiduciary duties that the LLC's members may have towards each other or to the LLC. Which of the following statements, if any, is correct?

(A) The LLC agreement can eliminate the members' liability for duty of care violations, but not the members' liability for duty of loyalty violations.

(B) The LLC agreement can eliminate the members' liability for duty of loyalty violations, but not the members' liability for duty of care violations.

(C) The LLC agreement can eliminate the members' liability for violating any fiduciary duty that the members may have towards each other or towards the LLC, but it cannot limit or eliminate a member's liability for any act or omission that constitutes a bad faith violation of the implied contractual covenant of good faith and fair dealing.

(D) None of the statements above is correct.

Facts for Question 12 (*)

Fred and George have formed a Delaware LLC. Fred wants to know whether he can assign half of his interest in the LLC to his brother Michael. Which, if any, of the following statements is correct.

(A) A member's interest in the LLC cannot be assigned to a third party without the consent of the LLC's other members.

(B) A member's interest in the LLC can be assigned to a third party without the consent of the other members, but only as a whole and not in part.

(C) A member's LLC can be assigned in whole or in part to a third party.

(D) None of the statements above is correct.

PART 2
ANSWERS

CHAPTER 5
AGENCY LAW

Answer to Question 1

(A) is the correct answer.

Under § 1.04(2)(b) of the Restatement (Third) of Agency, a "principal is undisclosed if, when an agent and a third party interact, the third party has no notice that the agent is acting for the principal." According to § 1.04(4), a person has notice of a fact "if the person knows the fact, has reason to know the fact, has received an effective notification of the fact, or should know the fact to fulfill the duty owed to another person." Applying this definition, we find that George, our third party, did not have notice of the fact that Ben was acting on Jennifer's behalf. Accordingly, Jennifer is an undisclosed principal. The fact that Ben should have disclosed Jennifer's involvement is immaterial.

(B) is incorrect.

Under § 1.04(2)(c) of the Restatement (Third) of Agency, a "principal is unidentified if, when an agent and a third party interact, the third party has notice that the agent is acting for a principal but does not have notice of the principal's identity." According to § 1.04(4), a person has notice of a fact "if the person knows the fact, has reason to know the fact, has received an effective notification of the fact, or should know the fact to fulfill the duty owed to another person." In the case at hand, George did not know and had no reason to know that the transaction involved anyone else but Ben. Therefore, Jennifer cannot be an unidentified principal.

(C) is incorrect.

Under § 1.04(2)(a) of the Restatement (Third) of Agency, a "principal is disclosed if, when an agent and a third party interact, the third party has notice that the agent is acting for a principal and has notice of the principal's identity." According to § 1.04(4), a person has notice of a fact "if the person knows the fact, has reason to know the fact, has received an effective notification of the fact, or should know the fact to fulfill the duty owed to another person." In the case at hand, George did not know and had no reason to know that the transaction involved anyone else but Ben. Therefore, Jennifer cannot be a disclosed principal.

(D) is incorrect.

According to § 2.03 of the Restatement (Third) of Agency, apparent authority requires that "a third party reasonably believes the actor has authority to act on behalf of the principal and that belief is traceable to the principal's manifestations." In the case at hand, George did not believe that Ben had authority to act for Jennifer. Accordingly, Ben did not act with apparent authority.

Answer to Question 2

(A) is the correct answer.

It is clear that a contract was formed because the agreement between Raphael and Casey was based on mutual assent and consideration. The decisive question, though, is whether that contract binds Peter. This depends on whether Raphael as Peter's agent has managed to bind Peter to the contract.

If you are faced with the question of whether an agent has bound the principal, you need to ask two questions. First, did the agent act on behalf of the principal in concluding the contract? And second, did the agent have the authority to bind the principal to that contract?

To determine whether the agent acted on behalf of the principal, you need to establish the principal's status. When dealing with a disclosed or unidentified principal, the question of whether the contract was entered into on behalf of the principal is determined from the perspective of the third party. The question, in other words, is how the third party could reasonably understand the agent's conduct. By contrast, what matters in the case of an undisclosed principal is the intention of the agent.

Under § 1.04(2)(a) of the Restatement (Third) of Agency, a "principal is disclosed if, when an agent and a third party interact, the third party has notice that the agent is acting for a principal and has notice of the principal's identity." Here, Casey had notice that Raphael was acting for Peter, so Peter was a disclosed principal. Accordingly, in determining whether Raphael was acting on Peter's behalf, we need to focus on Casey's (that is, the third party's) perspective. Given that Raphael had told Casey that he, Raphael, was acting for Peter, we therefore conclude that Raphael was acting on Peter's behalf.

The question remains whether Raphael had the necessary authority to bind Peter to the contract. Basically, the Restatement (Third) of Agency recognizes two types of authority that allow the agent to bind the principal, namely actual authority and apparent authority. Moreover, even if the agent has neither actual nor apparent authority to bind the principal, the principal may be bound as a result of estoppel or ratification. Under § 2.01 of the Restatement (Third) of Agency, "[a]n agent acts with actual authority when, at the time of taking action that has legal consequences for the principal, the agent reasonably believes, in accordance with the principal's manifestations to the agent, that the principal wishes the agent so to act." Here, Raphael knew that Peter wanted him to act as Peter's agent in buying the pizza. Therefore, Raphael had actual authority. Given that Raphael acted on Peter's behalf and had actual authority, a binding contract was formed between Peter and Casey.

(B) is incorrect.

Raphael acted with actual rather than apparent authority (see the answer to choice A).

(C) is incorrect.

Raphael had actual authority (see the answer to choice A).

(D) is incorrect.

The fact that Raphael secretly intended to conclude the contract for himself is immaterial (see the answer to choice A).

Answer to Question 3

(B) is the correct answer.

It is clear that a contract was formed because the agreement between Charlie and the car rental company involved both mutual assent and consideration. The decisive question, though, is whether and how that contract binds Arturo.

If you are faced with the question of whether an agent has bound the principal, you need to ask two questions. First, did the agent act on behalf of the principal in concluding the contract? And second, did the agent have the authority to bind the principal to that contract?

To determine whether the agent acted on behalf of the principal, you need to distinguish. When dealing with a disclosed or unidentified principal, the question of whether the contract was entered into on behalf of the principal is determined from the perspective of the third party. The question, in other words, is how the third party could reasonably understand the agent's conduct. By contrast, what matters in the case of an undisclosed principal is the intention of the agent.

Under § 1.04(2)(a) of the Restatement (Third) of Agency, "[a] principal is disclosed if, when an agent and a third party interact, the third party has notice that the agent is acting for a principal and has notice of the principal's identity." In the case at hand, Arturo's phone call to the car rental company ensured that the car rental agency had notice that Charlie was acting for Arturo, so Arturo was a disclosed principal. Accordingly, in determining whether Charlie was acting for Arturo, we have to focus on the car rental agency's perspective. Since the car rental agency knew that Charlie was acting for Arturo, we can conclude that Charlie was acting on Arturo's behalf.

The second question is whether and Charlie had the necessary authority to bind Arturo to the contract. The Restatement (Third) recognizes two types of authority that allow the agent to bind the principal, namely actual authority and apparent authority. Moreover, even if the agent has neither actual nor apparent authority to bind the principal, the principal may be bound as a result of estoppel or ratification. Under § 2.01 of the Restatement (Third) of Agency, "[a]n agent acts with actual authority when, at the time of taking action that has legal consequences for the principal, the agent reasonably believes, in accordance with the principal's manifestations to the agent, that the principal wishes the agent so to act." In the case at hand, Charlie had reasonable grounds for believing that Arturo wanted him to rent a car, but only a Ferrari, not a Bentley. Therefore, Charlie did not have actual authority to rent the Bentley.

What about apparent authority? According to § 2.03 of the Restatement (Third) of Agency, apparent authority requires that "a third party reasonably believes the actor has authority to act on behalf of the principal and that belief is traceable to the principal's manifestations." Given that Arturo had called ahead and told the rental agency that Charlie was authorized to rent any luxurious cars, these requirements are met. Therefore, Charlie acted with apparent authority.

(A) is incorrect.

In the case at hand, Charlie acted with apparent rather than actual authority (see the answer to choice B).

(C) is incorrect.

Charlie had apparent authority (see the answer to choice B). Therefore, there was no room for ratification.

(D) is incorrect.

Charlie had apparent authority (see the answer to choice B).

Answer to Question 4

(D) is the correct answer.

It is clear that a contract was formed because the agreement signed by Dylan and Marcus was based on mutual assent and consideration. Also, the contract was in writing and signed by both parties, such that the writing requirement in § 2–201 of the Uniform Commercial Code for sales contracts for $500 or more was satisfied. The question, though, is whether Nyusha can derive any rights from this contract.

A contract entered into by the agent binds the principal if the agent acted on behalf of the principal and with the authority to bind the principal. In this case, Dylan acted on behalf of the principal (for a closer analysis of the relevant principles see the answer to question 2). But did Dylan have the necessary authority?

Under § 2.01 of the Restatement (Third) of Agency, "[a]n agent acts with actual authority when, at the time of taking action that has legal consequences for the principal, the agent reasonably believes, in accordance with the principal's manifestations to the agent, that the principal wishes the agent so to act." In the case at hand, Dylan knew full well that Nyusha did not want her to buy any horses, so Dylan did not have actual authority.

What about apparent authority? Under § 2.03 of the Restatement (Third) of Agency, apparent authority requires that "a third party reasonably believes the actor has authority to act on behalf of the principal and that belief is traceable to the principal's manifestations." In the case at hand, Nyusha had not done anything that would suggest to Marcus that Dylan had authority to buy horses. Accordingly, Dylan did not have apparent authority either.

Even in the absence of authority, the contract binds the principal if the principal ratifies the contract. Ratification occurs where the principal's conduct justifies the assumption that the principal wants to be bound by the act undertaken by the agent. However, in order for this to be effective, the relevant act must be ratifiable (§ 4.03 of the Restatement (Third) of Agency), the principal must have capacity to ratify (§ 4.04), ratification must occur in a timely manner (§ 4.05), and the ratification must encompass the act in its entirety (§ 4.07). In the case at hand, this last requirement is not met since Nyusha only wanted to ratify part of the contract. (Note: If Dylan had entered into two contracts on Nyusha's behalf, then Nyusha could have ratified one but not the other. But in the case at hand, there was only one contract, and partial ratification is not allowed). Moreover, if the agent has acted without actual or apparent authority, the other party has the right to withdraw from the contract. Once the other party has exercised her withdrawal right, ratification is no longer timely (cf. § 4.05(1) of the Restatement (Third) of Agency)).

A contract can also be binding on the principal as a result of estoppel, but in order for estoppel to apply, the other party (in this case Marcus) has to invoke it. Marcus, however, does not want to be bound to the contract. In sum, Nyusha does not have any contractual rights against Marcus.

(A) is incorrect.

Dylan did not have actual authority (see the answer to choice D).

(B) is incorrect.

Dylan did not have apparent authority (see the answer to choice D).

(C) is incorrect.

Nyusha did not ratify the contract (see the answer to choice D).

Answer to Question 5

(A) is the correct answer.

It is clear that a contract was formed because the contract was based on mutual assent and consideration (the promise to deliver ten books in exchange for the promise to pay $300). Also note that the total price was not high enough to subject the contract to the writing requirement in § 2–201 of the Uniform Commercial Code for sales contracts for $500 or more. (In any case, once goods have been delivered and accepted, the contract is enforceable even if it was not in writing, UCC § 2-201(3)(c).)

But is Fatima bound by this contract? Maya is Fatima's agent. When Fatima and Maya agreed that Maya should run the store, they created an agency relationship with Fatima as the principal and Maya as the agent, for their agreement meant that Maya should act on Fatima's behalf and subject to her control (cf. § 1.01 of the Restatement (Third) of Agency). A contract concluded by an agent binds the principal if the agent acted on behalf of the principal and with the necessary authority.

Did Maya act on behalf of Fatima when she concluded the contract with George? George had no reason to know that Maya was not the owner and operator of the bookstore. Accordingly, Fatima was an undisclosed principal (see § 1.04(2)(b) of the Restatement (Third) of Agency). In the case of an undisclosed principal, the question of whether the agent acted on behalf of the principal is resolved by determining the agent's intent at the time the contract was formed. When Maya ordered the books, she wanted to acquire them not for herself, but for the store, and hence for Fatima, so that Maya acted on Fatima's behalf.

The question remains whether Maya acted with authority. The Restatement (Third) of Agency recognizes both actual and apparent authority. Actual authority exists where "the agent reasonably believes, in accordance with the principal's manifestations to the agent, that the principal wishes the agent so to act" (see § 2.01 of the Restatement (Third) of Agency). In the case at hand, Fatima had asked Maya to "fill in" for her. Maya could reasonably understand this statement to mean that Fatima wanted her to run the store in the ordinary course of business, and this includes purchasing popular books for the store. Accordingly, Maya acted not only on behalf of Fatima, but also with actual authority, when she purchased the books for the store. It follows that Fatima is bound by the contract with George and hence personally liable.

What about Maya's liability? Under § 6.03 of the Restatement, where "an agent acting with actual authority makes a contract on behalf of an undisclosed principal," the agent also is a party to the contract. At first glance, this may seem slightly unfair, since the third party can now hold two parties liable—the principal and the agent. Upon closer inspection, however, this makes a lot of sense since the third party reasonably believed that the agent was the other party and therefore should be able to hold that agent liable. Since Fatima is an undisclosed principal, this means that Maya, as her agent, remains a party to the contract and is therefore liable to George.

(B) is incorrect.

Both Fatima and Maya are liable to George (see the answer to choice A).

(C) is incorrect.

Both Fatima and Maya are liable to George (see the answer to choice A).

(D) is incorrect.

Both Fatima and Maya are liable to George (see the answer to choice A).

Answer to Question 6

(C) is the correct answer.

Both Kenji and Genevieve are liable to Travis. As regards Kenji, he is liable to Travis because he has committed a tort (negligence). The fact that Kenji acted as Genevieve's employee does not remove his own liability for torts that he commits (cf. § 7.01 of the Restatement (Third) of Agency, which notes that "an agent is subject to liability to a third party harmed by the agent's tortious conduct.").

Genevieve is also liable to Travis. Her liability is based on the theory of respondeat superior. As noted in § 7.07(1) of the Restatement (Third) of Agency), "[a]n employer is subject to vicarious liability for a tort committed by its employee acting within the scope of employment." Furthermore, "[a]n employee acts within the scope of employment when performing work assigned by the employer or engaging in a course of conduct subject to the employer's control," § 7.07(2) of the Restatement (Third) of Agency). By contrast, an "employee's act is not within the scope of employment when it occurs within an independent course of conduct not intended by the employee to serve any purpose of the employer," § 7.07(2) of the Restatement (Third) of Agency). In the case at hand, Kenji committed the tort while performing a task assigned to him by Genevieve (getting breakfast), and he was subject to her control, given that she was able to give him instructions. Kenji had not engaged in any independent course of conduct, and the breakfast run was in fact intended to serve his employer's purpose. Accordingly, Kenji was in fact acting within the scope of his employment, which meant that Genevieve was personally liable.

(A) is incorrect.

Both Kenji and Genevieve are liable (see the answer to choice C).

(B) is incorrect.

Both Kenji and Genevieve are liable (see the answer to choice C).

(D) is incorrect.

Both Kenji and Genevieve are liable (see the answer to choice C).

Answer to Question 7

(B) is the correct answer.

Let's focus, first, on the contract in the amount of $5,500,000. Mutual assent and consideration requirements are satisfied. Moreover, we do not have to worry about the statute of frauds. Whereas real estate sales generally have to be in writing to be enforceable, even an oral real estate sale becomes enforceable once ownership of the land has been transferred.

The only question, therefore, is whether the contract binds Carl under the rules of agency law. Gino explicitly acted in Carl's name, but did he have authority?

Carl had only allowed Gino to bid up to $5,000,000, so Gino lacked actual authority within the meaning of § 2.01 of the Restatement (Third) of Agency. Furthermore, there was no apparent authority. Under § 2.03 of the Restatement (Third) of Agency, an agent acts with apparent authority "when a third party reasonably believes the actor has authority to act on behalf of the principal and that belief is traceable to the principal's manifestations." From the auctioneer's perspective, the only factor suggesting that Gino had the authority to bid $5,500,000 was the fact that Gino actually bid this amount. And this action is not traceable to the principal's manifestations since Carl had not authorized this bid. Admittedly, Gino had previously undertaken various purchases for Carl, but they were minor purchases and did not involve real estate, so even if the auctioneer knew of the relevant transactions, they did not justify the belief that Gino had the necessary authority to bid $5,500,000 for the ranch.

Even in the absence of actual or apparent authority, a transaction is binding on the principal if it has been ratified. Ratification occurs where the principal's conduct justifies the assumption that the principal wants to be bound by the act undertaken by the agent. However, in order for this to be effective, the relevant act must be ratifiable (§ 4.03 of the Restatement (Third) of Agency), the principal must have capacity to ratify (§ 4.04), ratification must occur in a timely manner (§ 4.05), and the ratification must encompass the act in its entirety (§ 4.07). In the case at hand, all of these requirements are met; in particular, Carl has made it very clear that he wants to be bound by the contract. Therefore, the contract in the amount of $5,500,000 binds Carl.

What about the second contract, the one in the amount of $500,000? As before, we have mutual consent and consideration. Moreover, the contract was in writing and therefore satisfies the statute of frauds. The question, though, is whether the contract binds Carl under the rules of agency law. As before Gino lacked actual authority because Carl had never indicated to Gino that Gino was authorized to sell any property. Furthermore, Gino lacked apparent authority since there was nothing in Carl's conduct that the third party, Louis, could interpret as meaning that Gino had authority. Carl did not ratify the sale either because he did not even know about it at first and flatly rejected it once it was brought to his attention. Finally, there are no factors suggesting that Carl might be estopped from asserting Gino's lack of authority. It follows that the $500,000 contract does not bind Carl.

(A) is incorrect.

Only the contract in the amount of $5,500,000 binds Carl (see the answer to choice B).

(C) is incorrect.

Only the contract in the amount of $5,500,000 binds Carl (see the answer to choice B).

(D) is incorrect.

Only the contract in the amount of $5,500,000 binds Carl (see the answer to choice B).

Answer to Question 8

(A) is the correct answer.

Let's start with the question of whether Gerard is liable to Susan. A contract was formed, given that mutual assent and consideration are present. But the question is whether that contract binds Gerard. Obviously, Joe lacked actual authority given that Gerard never indicated to Joe that Joe could buy the cars in Gerard's name. Moreover, Joe did not have apparent authority either since Gerard did not engage in any conduct from which Susan could draw the reasonable conclusion that Gerard had authorized Joe to act in Gerard's name. Furthermore, Gerard never ratified the transaction. Quite to the contrary, when Susan first contacted him, Gerard flatly refused.

But the question remains whether Gerard is estopped from asserting Joe's lack of authority. As noted in § 2.05 of the Restatement (Third) of Agency, "[a] person who has not made a manifestation that an actor has authority as an agent and who is not otherwise liable as a party to a transaction purportedly done by the actor on that person's account is subject to liability to a third party who justifiably is induced to make a detrimental change in position because the transaction is believed to be on the person's account, if (1) the person intentionally or carelessly caused such belief, or (2) having notice of such belief and that it might induce others to change their positions, the person did not take reasonable steps to notify them of the facts." Susan justifiably believed, based on what she had heard from other luxury car sellers, that Joe was Gerard's agent. Moreover, while Gerard cannot be blamed for causing that belief, he knew that the luxury car sellers believed Joe to be his agent and that they were likely to sell him cars and yet failed to intervene. Therefore, Gerard is liable to Susan.

How about Joe? Your common sense, at the very least, should suggest that he, too, must be liable. Indeed, as noted in § 6.10 of the Restatement (Third) of Agency, a person who acts in another's name without having authority, is liable to the third party. Therefore, Joe, too, is liable to Susan.

(B) is incorrect.

Both Gerard and Joe are liable to Susan (see the answer to choice A).

(C) is incorrect.

Both Gerard and Joe are liable to Susan (see the answer to choice A).

(D) is incorrect.

Both Gerard and Joe are liable to Susan (see the answer to choice A).

CHAPTER 6
PARTNERSHIP LAW

Answer to Question 1

(A) is the correct answer.

According to UPA § 15, RUPA § 306, all partners are jointly and severally liable for the debts of a partnership.

Has a partnership been formed? Under UPA § 6(1), RUPA § 202(a), the formation of a partnership requires (a) an association of two or more persons (b) to carry on a business (c) as co-owners (d) for profit. A law firm constitutes a business within the meaning of these provisions (cf. RUPA § 101(1)), and it is reasonable to assume that Reuben and Maria are intending to make a profit. Furthermore, Reuben and Maria are two persons forming an association. Moreover, the fact that the law firm had not opened its doors to the public is irrelevant. Rather, it is sufficient that the carrying on of a business is the purpose of the association. Hence, a partnership was created on January 1. Given that Reuben and Maria are partners in that partnership, they are both jointly and severally liable.

(B) is incorrect.

Maria is also liable (see the answer to choice A).

(C) is incorrect.

Reuben is also liable (see the answer to choice A).

(D) is incorrect.

Both Maria and Reuben are liable (see the answer to choice A).

Answer to Question 2

(B) is the correct answer.

According to UPA § 15, RUPA § 306, all partners are jointly and severally liable for the debts of the partnership. In the case at hand, the firm constitutes a partnership because Rosalind and Viola (and later Cordelia) formed an association of two or more persons to carry on a business as co-owners for profit (cf. UPA § 6(1), RUPA § 202(a)). Does the liability towards Will constitute a debt of the partnership? A partnership is liable for any wrongful act that a partner has committed either with authority or in the ordinary course of business of the partnership, UPA § 13, RUPA § 305(a). Given that the delivery of promotional materials was part of the company's ordinary course of business, the partnership is liable for the tort (negligence) that Rosalind committed when she caused the accident. It follows that Rosalind and Viola, at least, are jointly and severally liable.

But what about Cordelia? When she signed the agreement with Rosalind and Viola, she also became one of the partners (cf. RUPA § 401(i)). However, an incoming partner is not personally liable for "old debts," i.e., liabilities incurred before the new partner joined the partnership, UPA § 17, RUPA § 306(b). In other words, the creditor can lay his hands on all the partnership assets, even those contributed by the new partner, but the creditor cannot touch the personal assets of the incoming partner. In other words, Cordelia is not liable to Will.

(A) is incorrect.

Viola is also liable (see the answer to choice B).

(C) is incorrect.

Cordelia is not liable to Will (see the answer to choice B).

(D) is incorrect.

Rosalind and Viola are jointly and severally liable (see the answer to choice B).

Answer to Question 3

(C) is the correct answer.

According to RUPA § 401(a), each partner is deemed to have an account. Let us start with Alexei's account. In 2013, Alexei made a contribution in the amount of $15,000. Contributions are credited to the partner's account, RUPA § 401(a)(1). That same year, however, the partnership made a loss in the amount of $10,000. Because each partner has to bear a share of the losses equal to his share of the profits, RUPA § 401(b), and because Alexei was to get 30 percent of the profits, Alexei has to bear $3,000 of the 2008 loss. Under RUPA § 401(a)(2), each partner's account is charged with his share of the partnership losses, so the $3,000 are charged to his account. That leaves Alexei with 12,000 at the end of 2013.

In 2014, the partnership made a profit in the amount of $100,000, and under the distribution rule chosen by the partnership, Alexei gets $30,000 out of the $100,000. Accordingly, the $30,000 is credited to his account, RUPA § 401(a)(1). If one sums up these various entries, Alexei's account shows a positive balance of $42,000.

Ivan, of course, is in exactly the same position as Alexei, so Ivan's account will show the same entries as Alexei's account, leading to a positive balance of $42,000.

Dmitri's account, by contrast, looks somewhat different. In 2003, Dmitri also made a contribution of $15,000 which is credited to his account. However, because under the partnership agreement, Dmitri was to get 40 percent rather than 30 percent of the profits made by the partnership (and therefore has to bear an equal proportion of the losses, RUPA § 401(b), his account is charged with $4,000 rather than $3,000. Moreover, in 2013, Dmitri received a distribution in the amount of $5,000, and under RUPA § 401(b), distributions are charged to the partner's account. That leaves Dimitri with $6,000 at the end of 2013.

In 2014, Dmitri's account is credited with $40,000, namely his share of the profits, and charged with the amount of the distribution he received, i.e., $2,000. Accordingly, his account shows a positive balance of $44,000.

(A) is incorrect.

Dmitri's account shows a positive balance of $44,000 (see the answer to choice C).

(B) is incorrect.

Alexei's and Ivan's accounts each show a positive balance of $42,000; Dmitri's account shows a positive balance of $44,000 (see the answer to choice C).

(D) is incorrect.

Answer choice C is correct (see the answer to choice C).

Answer to Question 4

(B) is the correct answer.

Under UPA § 18(b), RUPA § 401(c), a partnership will reimburse a partner for payments made for the preservation of partnership property. In the case at hand, the repairs were necessary for the preservation of the partnership property, and Percy can therefore demand to be reimbursed.

(A) is incorrect.

Percy's claim against the partnership is based on partnership law, not on unjust enrichment (see the answer to choice B).

(C) is incorrect.

The fact that Percy had no role in the management of the partnership does not preclude him from asserting a claim under RUPA § 401(c).

(D) is incorrect.

Answer choice B is correct (see the answer to choice B).

Answer to Question 5

(A) is the correct answer.

Under UPA § 25(2)(a), RUPA § 401(g), a partner may possess partnership property only for partnership purposes. An exception applies where all other partners consent, but that was not the case here.

(B) is incorrect.

Had all three partners consented to the use of the car, then Percy would not have breached his duties as a partner (see the answer to choice A).

(C) is incorrect.

The consent of one of the other partners is insufficient (see the answer to choice A).

(D) is incorrect.

Answer choice A is correct (see the answer to choice A).

Answer to Question 6

(B) is the correct answer.

The general default rule is that each partner is allowed to undertake acts that are within the ordinary course of business of the partnership. However, under UPA § 18(h), RUPA § 401(j), differences arising regarding matters in the ordinary course of business of a partnership can be decided by a majority of the partners. In the case at hand, buying caviar is a matter in the ordinary course of business for a fine foods store. Accordingly, the matter could be decided by a simple majority of the partners. Hence, George and Fred did not violate their duties.

(A) is incorrect.

A decision regarding a matter in the ordinary course of the partnership's business does not have to be unanimous (see the answer to choice B).

(C) is incorrect.

As a general rule, each partner is allowed to undertake acts that are within the ordinary course of business of the partnership. However, under UPA § 18(h), RUPA § 401(j), differences arising regarding matters in the ordinary course of business of a partnership can be decided by a majority of the partners; and once a matter has been decided, that decision has to be respected by all partners.

(D) is incorrect.

Answer choice B is correct (see the answer to choice B).

Answer to Question 7

(C) is the correct answer.

Under UPA § 18(e), RUPA § 401(f), the default rule is that all partners have "equal rights in the management and conduct of the partnership business." While the partnership agreement can deviate from this principle, there are no indications that the agreement between Percy, George, and Fred opted out of the legal default. Moreover, in order to amend the partnership agreement, a unanimous consensus among the partners is needed. This is explicitly stated in RUPA § 401(j), and the same is true under the Uniform Partnership Act (1914).

(A) is incorrect.

See the answer to choice C.

(B) is incorrect.

See the answer to choice C.

(D) is incorrect.

Answer choice C is correct (see the answer to choice C).

Answer to Question 8

(C) is the correct answer.

Under UPA § 18(g), RUPA § 401(i), the general default rule is that a person can only become a partner with the consent of all existing partners. Given that Percy refuses to agree to Ginevra's admission to the partnership, she cannot become a partner.

(A) is incorrect.

The admission of new partners requires unanimity (see the answer to choice C).

(B) is incorrect.

The admission of new partners requires unanimity (see the answer to choice C).

(D) is incorrect.

Answer choice C is correct (see the answer to choice C).

Answer to Question 9

(A) is the correct answer.

Under RUPA § 403(b), a partner has the right to inspect the partnership's books. RUPA § 403(b) also makes it clear that the partner's "agents and attorneys" may inspect the book as well. Moreover, these rights cannot be "unreasonably restricted", RUPA § 103(b)(2). Accordingly, the provision in the partnership agreement that prohibits partners other than Lucan from inspecting the books is void.

(B) is incorrect.

A partner can demand that his attorney be given access to the partnership's books (see the answer to choice A).

(C) is incorrect.

A partner has the right to inspect the partnership's books (see the answer to choice A).

(D) is incorrect.

Both the partner and his attorney(s) must be given access to the partnership's books (see the answer to choice A).

Answer to Question 10

(A) is the correct answer.

Note, first, that the firm is a partnership because Thelma and Louise have formed an association of two persons to carry on a for-profit business as co-owners, RUPA § 202(a). A partnership is dissolved when its business becomes illegal, RUPA § 801(4). Accordingly, the first statute caused the dissolution of the partnership. However, under RUPA § 801(4), "a cure of illegality within 90 days after notice of the partnership of the event is effective retroactive to the date of the event for purposes of this section." In other words, if the business becomes legal again within 90 days, then we treat the partnership as though it had never been dissolved. In the case at hand, only 30 days passed between the two laws, meaning that the firecracker store partnership is treated as though it had never been dissolved.

(B) is incorrect.

While the first statute made the partnership business illegal and thereby caused the dissolution of the partnership, the second statute was adopted within 90 days, so that the partnership is treated as though it had never been dissolved (see the answer to choice A).

(C) is incorrect.

The second statute was adopted within 90 days, so that the partnership is treated as though it had never been dissolved (see the answer to choice A).

(D) is incorrect.

Answer D overlooks the fact that the first statute made the partnership business illegal and thereby caused the dissolution of the partnership under RUPA § 801(4).

Answer to Question 11

(D) is the correct answer.

According to RUPA § 601(3), a partner may be expelled from the partnership pursuant to a provision in the partnership agreement. The UPA contains no explicit rule of this type, but the same principle applies under the UPA since the partners are free to shape the internal structure of the partnership via agreement. Here, Moe and Bearle have made use of their right to expel Larry, and there is no indication that they violated their fiduciary duties in doing so.

(A) is incorrect.

See the answer to choice D.

(B) is incorrect.

See the answer to choice D.

(C) is incorrect.

See the answer to choice D.

Answer to Question 12

(A) is the correct answer.

The formation of a partnership requires an association of two or more persons to carry on a for-profit business as co-owners, UPA § 6(1), RUPA 202(a). However, the term "person" is defined generously in this context. According to RUPA § 101(10), the term "person" includes, *inter alia*, an individual, a corporation, a trust, and a partnership. Under UPA § 2, the term "person" covers individuals, corporations, partnerships, and "other associations." Because a trust is another association within the meaning of this provision, it can be a partner under the UPA.

(B) is incorrect.

Under UPA § 2, RUPA § 101(10), a partnership is a person within the meaning of partnership law and can therefore be a partner in a partnership (see the answer to choice A).

(C) is incorrect.

Under UPA § 2, RUPA § 101(10), a trust is a person within the meaning of partnership law and can therefore be a partner in a partnership (see the answer to choice A).

(D) is incorrect.

Under UPA § 2, RUPA § 101(10), a corporation is a person within the meaning of partnership law and can therefore be a partner in a partnership (see the answer to choice A).

Answer to Question 13

(A) is the correct answer.

Because the partners had agreed on a minimum duration for their partnership, the partnership was a partnership for a definite term within the meaning of UPA § 31(1)(a), RUPA § 801(2). (After ten months, the partnership would have transformed into an at-will-partnership within the meaning of UPA § 31(1)(b), RUPA §§ 101(8), 801(1). However, even partnerships for a definite term can be dissolved before the expiration of that term. In particular, a partnership for a definite term can be dissolved by unanimous agreement of the partners, UPA § 31(1)(c), RUPA § 801(2)(ii). On January 20, all three of the partners consented to the dissolution of the partnership. Therefore, the partnership was dissolved that day.

(B) is incorrect.

The partnership had already been dissolved on January 20, 2014 (see the answer to choice A). Moreover, under the RUPA, the death of a partner does not dissolve the partnership if at least two other partners remain; rather, the partner's death will only cause that partner's dissociation from the partnership under RUPA § 601(7)(i). The old UPA (1914) takes a different approach. Under the UPA, the death of any partner dissolves the partnership under UPA § 31(4). However, in the case at hand, the partnership could not be dissolved under UPA § 31(4), because it had already been dissolved earlier by unanimous resolution of the partners.

(C) is incorrect.

The partnership had already been dissolved on January 20, 2014 (see the answer to choice A). If the partnership had not been dissolved by unanimous consent on January 20, then the timing of the dissolution would have depended on whether the partnership is governed by the Revised Uniform Partnership Act (1997)—the RUPA—or the older Uniform Partnership Act (1914)—the UPA:

Under the RUPA, Sandy's death on January 25 would have been insufficient to dissolve the partnership (see the answer to choice A). By contrast, Brad's death would have dissolved the partnership, for even though the general rule is that dead partners are only dissociated under RUPA § 601(7)(i), a partnership needs to consist of at least two persons, RUPA § 202(a), and the partnership is therefore dissolved when only one partner remains.

Under the UPA, the death of any partner will dissolve the partnership under UPA § 31(4). Accordingly, if the partnership had not already been dissolved on January 20, 2014, it would have been dissolved by Sandy's death on January 25, 2014.

(D) is incorrect.

The partnership was dissolved on January 20, 2014 (see the answer to choice A).

Answer to Question 14

(B) is the correct answer.

First note that this was a partnership because the four musicians formed an association to carry on, as co-owners, a for-profit business, UPA § 6, RUPA § 202(a). Furthermore, because the four musicians had agreed to stay together for at least as long as it would take to complete the tour, the partnership was for a definite term or undertaking within the meaning of UPA § 31(1)(a), RUPA § 801(2).

The question of when the partnership was dissolved depends on whether the case is governed by the 1997 RUPA or by the old 1914 UPA. Under the RUPA, the death of a partner does not dissolve the partnership if at least two other partners remain; rather, the partner's death will only cause that partner's dissociation from the partnership under RUPA § 601(7)(i). Under the old UPA (1914), the death of any partner will dissolve the partnership under UPA § 31(4). Given that the question stipulates that the case is governed by the RUPA, the partnership was not dissolved when Keith died.

However, Keith's death is nonetheless important. According to RUPA § 801(2)(i), a partnership for a definite term or particular undertaking is dissolved if, within 90 days after a partner's dissociation by death, at least half of the remaining partners express their wish to wind up the partnership business. In the case at hand, only three partners remained after Keith's death, and two of them wanted to wind up the partnership business. Accordingly, the partnership was dissolved when Charlie and Ron declared that they wanted to wind up the business.

Note that if Charlie and Ron had not declared their wish to wind up the partnership business, then the partnership would not have been dissolved at all, not even when Ron died. As previously noted, under the RUPA, the death of a partner does not dissolve the partnership if at least two other partners remain, and that was the case here, because even after Keith and Ron died, Mick and Charlie remained.

(A) is incorrect.

Under the RUPA, the death of a partner does not dissolve the partnership if at least two partners remain. See the answer to choice B.

(C) is incorrect.

By the time that Ron died, the partnership had already been dissolved, and in any case, under the RUPA, the death of a partner does not dissolve the partnership if at least two partners remain. See the answer to choice B.

(D) is incorrect.

The partnership was dissolved when Charlie and Ron declared that they wanted to wind up the business. See the answer to choice B.

Answer to Question 15

(B) is the correct answer.

As a general rule, each partner has the authority to enter into transactions in the normal course of the partnership business, and her actions bind the partnership vis-à-vis third parties, UPA § 9(1), RUPA § 301(1). Within the partnership agreement, the authority of some or all of the partners can be curtailed. However, even when the partnership limits the authority of the partners, the partner may still be able to bind the partnership vis-à-vis third parties, cf. UPA § 9, RUPA § 301. In other words, the fact that the partner was not *allowed* to act for the partnership does not necessarily mean that his actions don't bind the partnership. To what extent third parties are protected in this situation depends on whether it is the RUPA or the UPA which applies.

Under the UPA, an act "for apparently carrying on in the usual way the business of the partnership" binds the partnership unless the third party "has knowledge of the fact" that the partner lacks authority, § 9(1) UPA. Under the RUPA, an act "for apparently carrying on in the ordinary course the partnership business" binds the partnership unless the third party "knew or had received a notification that the partner lacked authority," RUPA § 301(1). In the case at hand, the purchase was a typical purchase for a bookstore, and Willow neither knew nor had received notification that Giles lacked authority to enter into the transaction. Therefore, the contract binds the partnership regardless of whether one applies the RUPA or the UPA.

But what about the statement of partnership authority? Whereas the UPA does not provide for such statements, the RUPA gives the partners the option of filing a statement of partnership authority which may describe the limitations on the authority of the partners, RUPA § 303(a)(2). As a general rule, though, a third party is not deemed to know of a limitation on authority simply because that limitation is mentioned in a statement of partnership authority, RUPA § 303(f). The only exception to this rule concerns the transfer of real estate: under RUPA § 303(e), "a person not a partner is deemed to know of a limitation on the authority of a partners to transfer real property held in the name of the partnership if a certified copy of the filed statement containing the limitation on authority is of record in the office for recording transfers of that real property." In the case at hand, the transaction had nothing to do with real estate, so that the statement of partnership authority could not be invoked to Willow's detriment.

(A) is incorrect.

The partnership agreement can—and often does—limit the authority of the partners. Whether such limitations prevent the acting partner from binding the partnership is another question and one that depends on the circumstances and the nature of the transaction, cf. UPA § 9, RUPA § 301.

(C) is incorrect.

Except in certain cases involving the transfer of real estate, a third party is not deemed to know of a limitation on authority simply because that limitation is contained in a statement of partnership authority (see the answer to choice B).

(D) is incorrect.

See the answer to choice B.

Answer to Question 16

(A) is the correct answer.

Note, first, that the firm is a partnership because Harry and Sally have formed an association of two persons to carry on a for-profit business as co-owners, UPA § 6(1), RUPA § 202(a). If these conditions are met, the partnership is formed regardless of whether the partners wanted to form a partnership. This is expressly noted in RUPA § 202(a), but is true under the UPA as well. In particular, the fact that the parties called their firm a "joint venture" does not prevent the formation of a partnership. Also note that Harry is in fact a partner rather than, say, a mere lender. Harry and Sally were to share the profits, so the presumption in favor of a partnership under RUPA § 202(c)(3) applies. The mere fact that Sally alone was to bear any loss is insufficient to rebut that presumption. Hence, all of the conditions for the formation of a partnership are satisfied.

Sally created a partnership liability when she took on the loan. The allocation of authority in a partnership is determined, first and foremost, by the partnership agreement, RUPA § 103(a). If the partnership agreement is silent, then each partner has the authority to enter into transactions in the normal course of the partnership business. When, in the ordinary course of business, a difference arises between the partners regarding some matter, that matter can be decided by a simple majority, UPA § 18(h), RUPA § 401(j). How that rule applies when there are only two partners is controversial; courts disagree regarding whether a partner has authority to undertake a transaction if the only other party has indicated that he opposes the relevant transaction. In the case at hand, however, this controversy is without relevance. That is because the partnership agreement explicitly gives Sally the authority to obtain loans of up to $200,000 for the partnership, and Harry cannot unilaterally eliminate this authority. Rather, the partnership agreement can only be changed with the consent of all the partners. It follows that Sally had the authority necessary to obtain the loan, and her actions therefore bound the partnership under UPA § 9(1), RUPA § 301(1).

As a general rule, the partners are jointly and severally liable for all of the partnership's debts, RUPA § 306(a). The UPA imposes joint liability for contractual obligations of the partnership, UPA § 15(b). Either way, each partner is liable for the full amount, though the bank cannot obtain the full amount more than once. Moreover, the provision in the partnership agreement according to which only Sally shall be personally liable has no effect vis-à-vis the bank. While RUPA § 306(a) allows the partners to limit their personal liability via an agreement with the creditor, mere agreements *between the partners* cannot limit the partners' liability vis-à-vis third parties. In sum, Harry is personally liable for the full amount.

(B) is incorrect.

Partners are jointly and severally liable, RUPA § 306(a), meaning that Harry is liable for the full amount (see the answer to choice A).

(C) is incorrect.

The firm is a partnership because Harry and Sally have formed an association of two persons to carry on as co-owners a for-profit business, UPA § 6(1), RUPA § 202(a) (see the answer to choice A). Whether they intended to form a partnership does not matter.

(D) is incorrect.

Given that the partnership agreement explicitly granted Sally the necessary authority, the fact that Harry opposed the loan was irrelevant (see the answer to choice A).

Answer to Question 17

(C) is the correct answer.

Note, first, that the firm is a partnership because Bruce, Arnold, Denzel, Jackie and Sylvester have formed an association of five persons to carry on a for-profit business as co-owners, UPA § 6(1), RUPA § 202(a).

This partnership was dissolved regardless of whether one applies the RUPA or the UPA. The timing of the dissolution does, however, depend on whether it is the UPA or the RUPA that is applicable. The death of any partner will dissolve the partnership under UPA § 31(4). Under the RUPA however, the death of a partner does not dissolve the partnership if at least two other partners remain; rather, the partner's death will only cause that partner's dissociation from the partnership under RUPA § 601(7)(i). In other words, Bruce's death would have dissolved the partnership if it were governed by the UPA, but since the RUPA applies, Bruce's death does not dissolve the partnership. However, under RUPA § 801(2)(i), a partnership for a definite term or particular undertaking is dissolved if, within 90 days after a partner's dissociation by death, at least half of the remaining partners express their wish to wind up the partnership business. In the case at hand, four partners remained after Bruce's death, and two of them wanted to wind up the partnership business. Accordingly, under the RUPA, the partnership was dissolved when Arnold and Sylvester expressed their wish to wind up the partnership business.

The dissolution does not terminate the partnership. Rather, the partnership continues for the purpose of winding up the firm's business, UPA § 30, RUPA § 802(a). However, dissolution impacts the ability of the partners to bind the partnership. The rules of the UPA and the RUPA vary somewhat on the details of this impact, but the result is the same.

Under RUPA § 804(1), a partner can bind the partnership after it has been dissolved to the extent that (a) "the transaction is appropriate for winding up the partnership business." While some purchases, especially minor ones, may be completely appropriate for winding up a business, Jackie's purchase of 20 new tables does not fall into this category. However, under RUPA § 804(2), a partner can also bind the partnership after it has been dissolved if the third party did not have notice of the dissolution and if, before the dissolution, the contract would have been binding on the partnership under RUPA § 301. According to RUPA § 102(b), a person has notice of a fact if he knows the fact, has received notification of the fact, or has reason to know the fact. In the case at hand, Tom did not even have reason to know the fact and therefore did not have notice. The only question therefore, is whether the transaction would have bound the partnership under RUPA § 301 RUPA before the dissolution. Before the dissolution, each partner had the authority to enter into contracts in the ordinary course of business and such contracts were binding on the partnership under RUPA § 301(1). For a restaurant, buying tables qualifies as a transaction in the ordinary course of business. It follows, then, that Jackie's transaction would have bound the partnership before the dissolution and is therefore binding on the partnership under RUPA § 804(2).

If the case were governed by the UPA, the applicable rules would be slightly different. Under UPA § 35(1)(a), a partner can bind the partnership by "any act appropriate for winding up partnership affairs or completing transactions unfinished at dissolution." As previously noted though, the purchase of the tables cannot be characterized as a transaction for winding up the partnership business, and it did not serve the completion of unfinished transactions either. Under UPA § 35(1)(b), the partner can also bind the partnership by any transaction that would have bound the partnership prior to the dissolution. As under the RUPA, the UPA requires that the third party did not have notice of the and also imposes some additional requirements: either a) the third party must have "extended credit to the partnership prior to [its] dissolution," or b) the third party must both have "known of the partnership before [its] dissolution" and the dissolution must not have been "advertised in a newspaper of general circulation" in the place where "the partnership business was regularly carried on." In the case at hand, these requirements were met: Tom has in fact known the partnership since its formation, no newspaper mentioned the series of events that took place within the partnership, and Tom had no reason to know of the dissolution. Matters get a little more complicated though, because the UPA imposes some additional limitations on the protection of third parties. First, the partnership is not bound by contracts concluded after the dissolution, if the partnership was dissolved because its business became illegal. Of course, that is not the case here. Rather, under the UPA, the partnership was dissolved because Bruce died. Second, subject to certain exceptions, the third party is not protected if the partner who concluded the contract became bankrupt, UPA § 35(3)(b). In the case at hand, that's not a problem either since nothing in the facts suggests that Jackie has become bankrupt. Third, as a general rule, the contract fails to bind the partnership if the partner who concluded the contract did not have authority to wind up the partnership business. To determine whether Jackie had authority to wind up the partnership business, we have to look to UPA § 37. Under that provision, the default rule is that every partner who has not wrongfully dissolved the partnership and is not bankrupt has the right to wind up the partnership's business. Accordingly, Jackie did have the authority for winding up the firm's affairs. In sum, even under the UPA, Jackie managed to bind the partnership.

(A) is incorrect.

Dissolution does not terminate the partnership, UPA § 30, RUPA § 802(a), and Jackie did in fact manage to bind the partnership (see the answer to choice C).

(B) is incorrect.

Admittedly, the dissolution of the partnership terminates the partners' authority for all acts that are not part of winding up the partnership, cf. UPA § 33, RUPA § 803. Moreover, Jackie's purchase could not be qualified as appropriate for winding up the partnership business. However, Jackie nonetheless managed to bind the partnership under the rules designed to protect third parties in case of dissolution (see the answer to choice C).

(D) is incorrect.

The partnership was in fact dissolved. If the partnership was governed by the UPA then, under UPA § 31(4), the dissolution occurred when Bruce died. If the partnership was governed by the RUPA then, under RUPA § 801(2)(1), the dissolution occurred when half of the remaining partners declared their intent to wind up the partnership business.

Answer to Question 18

(D) is the correct answer.

Note, first, that the firm is a partnership because Dolly, Emmylou, Loretta and Patsy have formed an association of two persons to carry on as co-owners a business for profit, RUPA § 202(a). Under RUPA § 601(1), a partner can dissociate at any time by declaring her will to withdraw. In the case at hand, Dolly has made it clear that she no longer wants to be part of the partnership, and has thereby dissociated herself from the partnership.

This dissociation has not dissolved the partnership. Admittedly, because the partners have not specified a particular term or undertaking, the partnership is a partnership at will, and a partnership at will is normally dissolved when any of the partners notifies the partnership of his will to withdraw as a partner, RUPA § 801(1). However, under RUPA § 103, that rule is only a default rule. Accordingly, the partnership agreement could (and in this case did) provide that the dissociation did not dissolve the partnership. (Note, however, that the dissociation of a partner always dissolves the partnership when less than two partners remain after the dissociation, because, under RUPA § 202(a), a partnership always requires at least two partners.)

Once a partner has dissociated without causing the partnership's dissolution, the partnership has to purchase the dissociated partner's partnership interest. Under RUPA § 701(b), the buyout price is "the amount that would have been distributable to the dissociating partner under RUPA 807(b) if, on the date of the dissociation, the assets of the partnership were sold at a price equal to the greater of the liquidation value or the value based on the entire business as a going concern without the dissociated partner and the partnership were wound up as of that date." RUPA § 807(b) is tailored to a case in which the partnership has been dissolved and provides that, upon winding up the partnership business, the accounts must be settled and each partner is entitled to distribution in an amount equal to any excess of the charges over the credits in the partner's account.

What does Dolly's account look like? The $10,000 that she has contributed are credited to Dolly's account, RUPA § 401(a)(1). However, the $10,000 that were later distributed to Dolly have to be charged to her account, RUPA § 401(a)(2), meaning that the net balance of distributions and contributions is zero.

Also credited to the partner's account are profits, whereas losses are charged, RUPA § 401(a). This includes profits and losses from the liquidation of the business in the winding-up phase. As a legal default, each partner is entitled to an equal share of the profits and losses, RUPA § 401(b). While the facts do not describe the losses and profits in detail, it does mention that, overall, the restaurant is worth $1,000,000 (going concern value) or $400,000 (liquidation value). Hence, after summing up the profits and losses, Dolly's share in case of a sale of the restaurant, would be $250,000 (going concern value) or $100,000 (liquidation value). Hence, if the partnership were dissolved and the restaurant sold, Dolly could expect a distribution in the amount of either $250,000 (going concern value) or $100,000 (liquidation value). Since RUPA § 701(b) declares the higher of these two prices to be decisive in calculating the buyout price, Dolly can expect a buyout price in the amount of $250,000.

(A) is incorrect.

Even without any stipulation in the partnership agreement, the partner has the right to receive the appropriate buyout price for this partnership interest, RUPA § 701(a).

(B) is incorrect.

Under UPA § 701(a), RUPA § 807(b), the buyout price paid to the dissociated partner takes into account not only the contributions that the partner has made, but also the distributions that she has received as well as her share of the losses and profits.

(C) is incorrect.

Dolly could expect a payment of $100,000 if the buyout price were based on the liquidation value, but under RUPA § 701(a), the buyout price is based on the higher of the liquidation value and the going concern value.

Answer to Question 19

(D) is the correct answer.

Note, first, that the firm is a partnership because Hank, Conway, Buck and Johnny have formed an association of two or more persons to carry on a for-profit business as co-owners, RUPA § 202(a). Moreover, the loan constitutes a partnership liability. Hank acted with authority when he obtained the loan for the firm, and his actions bind the partnership, RUPA § 301. All partners are jointly and severally liable for debts of the partnership, RUPA § 306(1).

Furthermore, the fact that Buck dissociated from the partnership did not eliminate his liability as a partner, RUPA § 703(a). However, under RUPA § 703(d), a "partner is released from liability for a partnership obligation if a partnership creditor, with notice of the partner's dissociation but without the partner's consent, agrees to a material alteration in the nature or time of payment of a partnership obligation." In the case at hand, Bank Corp. knew that Buck had left the partnership, and, without Buck's consent, agreed to change the time of payment by one year. Therefore, Buck was released from his liability for the loan under RUPA § 703(d). Hence the bank cannot hold Buck liable at all. For many students, this provision is somewhat counterintuitive. They assume that the dissociated partner cannot be held liable for the alteration of the debt—in this case the additional $10,000—but still want to hold him liable for the original amount. However, the release under RUPA § 703(d) covers the original debt as well. This makes sense if you consider that if the debt had not been modified, it would have come due earlier and might already have been paid.

(A) is incorrect.

Buck has been fully released from his liability under RUPA § 703(d) (see the answer to choice D).

(B) is incorrect.

Buck has been fully released from his liability under RUPA § 703(d) (see the answer to choice D).

(C) is incorrect.

Buck has been fully released from his liability under RUPA § 703(d) (see the answer to choice D).

Answer to Question 20

(A) is the correct answer.

Note, first, that the firm is a partnership because Charlotte, Emily, Anne, and Branwell have formed an association of two or more persons to carry on as co-owners a business for profit, RUPA § 202(a). The big question is whether

Charlotte created a partnership liability when she purchased the tofu from Elizabeth. For dissociated partners, the power to bind the partnership is governed by RUPA § 702. Under that provision, a dissociated partner retains the power to bind the partnership for two years after leaving the partnership, if certain conditions are met.

To begin, the dissociated partner can only bind the partnership if the relevant act would have bound the partnership prior to the dissociation. For a vegetarian restaurant, buying tofu is a standard transaction, and every partner has the authority to enter into contracts in the ordinary course of business. Therefore, if Charlotte had purchased the tofu before her dissociation, she would have been acting with authority, and the transaction would have bound the partnership, RUPA § 301.

Furthermore, for the dissociated partner to bind the partnership under RUPA § 702, the other party to the transaction must have reasonably believed that the dissociated partner was still a partner and must not have had notice of the dissociation. In the case at hand, Elizabeth reasonably thought that Charlotte was still a partner and had no reason to know of the dissociation. Note, in this context, that the mere fact that a statement of dissociation has been filed does not mean that third parties have notice of the dissociation.

Finally, the dissociated partner can only bind the partnership if the third party was not deemed to know of the dissociation under RUPA § 704(c). Under that provision, third parties are "deemed to have notice of the dissociation 90 days after the statement dissociation is filed." In the case at hand, a statement of dissociation was filed, but at the time that the contract was concluded, 90 days had not yet passed. It follows, therefore, that Charlotte managed to bind the partnership and thereby create a partnership liability. Under RUPA § 306(1), all partners are jointly and severally liable for the relevant debt.

(B) is incorrect.

If Elizabeth had known about the dissociation then Charlotte would not have been able to bind the partnership, RUPA § 702(d).

(C) is incorrect.

Emily is in fact liable (see the answer to choice A). The statement of dissociation did not prevent the creation of this liability because the contract was formed less than 90 days after the statement was filed, cf. RUPA § 704(c).

(D) is incorrect.

Emily is in fact liable (see the answer to choice A).

Answer to Question 21

(C) is the correct answer.

Note, first, that the firm is a partnership because Will, Jill, Hester, Chester, Peter, Polly, Tim, Tom, Mary, Larry, and Clarinda have formed an association of two or more persons to carry on as co-owners a business for profit, RUPA § 202(a). The decisive question is whether the events that occurred between January 1 and January 20 led to the dissolution of the partnership and/or to the dissociation of one or more partners.

The RUPA lists all dissolving events in RUPA § 801. However, none of the events listed there have occurred in the case at hand. Admittedly, under RUPA § 801(5), the partnership can be dissolved if "another partner has engaged in conduct relating to the partnership business which makes it not reasonably practicable to carry on the business in partnership with that partner." In the case at hand, both Clarinda, who stole from the partnership, and Peter, who sold the partnership's secrets to a competitor, can be argued to have engaged in conduct which satisfies this condition. However, under RUPA § 801(5), the partnership's dissolution does not occur automatically. Rather, it takes a judicial determination in order to dissolve the partnership. Since there was no such judicial determination, the partnership was not dissolved.

The remaining question concerns whether any of the partners were dissociated from the partnership. Dissociating events are listed in RUPA § 601. Needless to say, marrying is not a ground for dissociation, so Tom is still a partner.

Events that automatically cause the partnership's dissolution, without any need for a formal judicial determination, include the death of a partner (RUPA § 601(7)(i)), the appointment of a guardian (RUPA § 601(7)(ii)), and the partner's becoming a debtor in bankruptcy (RUPA § 607(6)(i)). Hence, Larry, Tim, and Polly were dissociated from the partnership. Furthermore, a partner is automatically dissociated from the partnership in case of "the partner's expulsion pursuant to the partnership agreement," RUPA § 601(3). The other partners tried to expel Clarinda, but this attempt at expelling her did not have any basis in the partnership agreement and therefore did not lead to her dissociation.

Under RUPA § 605(i), a partner can be expelled because he has engaged in "wrongful conduct that [has] adversely and materially affected the partnership business," and under RUPA § 605(ii) the same is true if the partner has "willfully and persistently" breached his duty of loyalty to the other partners in a material way. In the case at hand, both Clarinda's repeated theft and Peter's sale of the partnership's secret can be argued to satisfy these requirements. However, RUPA § 601(b) requires a judicial determination on application by a partner, and, in the case at hand, no such judicial determination has taken place. Hence, despite their misdeeds, Clarinda and Peter are still part of the partnership.

In sum, the only partners who were dissociated are Larry, Tim, and Polly. That leaves Will, Jill, Hester, Chester, Peter, Tom, Mary, and Clarinda.

(A) is incorrect.

The partnership was never dissolved because none of the dissolving events listed in RUPA § 801 are present (see the answer to choice C).

(B) is incorrect.

The partnership was never dissolved because none of the dissolving events listed in RUPA § 801 are present (see the answer to choice C).

(D) is incorrect.

Clarinda was not dissociated from the partnership because the attempt of the other partners to expel her lacked a basis in the partnership agreement (see the answer to choice C).

Answer to Question 22

(D) is the correct answer.

According to UPA § 18(b), RUPA § 401(c), the partnership has to reimburse partners for payments made in the ordinary course of the partnership business. Note that paying partnership liabilities is part of the ordinary course of business, such that Chandler has a right to be reimbursed if he discharged a partnership liability by paying Ross. A partnership is liable for any wrongful act that a partner has committed either with authority or in the ordinary course of business of the partnership, UPA § 13, RUPA § 305. Here, Chandler caused the accident when he was driving to a supplier to pick up bikes, and so he committed the tort (negligence) in the ordinary course of business. Accordingly, Ross's tort claim was a partnership liability, so that paying that liability created a right to reimbursement.

But what about the fact that Chandler acted negligently? Under RUPA § 404(a), the partners owe the partnership and each other a duty of care. The older UPA does not explicitly mention such a duty, but there is nonetheless wide agreement that partners owe the partnership a duty of care. Could one argue that Chandler violated that duty and therefore owed the partnership damages—a claim that the partnership could offset against Chandler's claim for reimbursement? The answer is no. While the partners owe the partnership a duty of care, that duty "is limited to refraining from engaging in grossly negligent or reckless conduct, intentional misconduct, or a knowing violation of the law," RUPA § 404(c). The same is true under the UPA. Because Chandler only acted with simple negligence, he did not breach his duty of care. Hence, he can demand to be reimbursed by the partnership.

(A) is incorrect.

Chandler's right to be reimbursed follows from UPA § 18(b), RUPA § 401(c). Hence, it does not matter that the partnership agreement does not grant him a right to reimbursement.

(B) is incorrect.

Chandler's negligence does not bar him from demanding reimbursement (see the answer to choice D).

(C) is incorrect.

The partnership is in fact liable to Ross (see the answer to choice D).

Answer to Question 23

(D) is the correct answer.

Let us start with the question of whether the partnership is liable. Note, first, that Lisa, Mary and Nora formed a partnership when they started the bookstore, because they formed an association of two or more persons to carry on as co-owners a business for profit, UPA § 6, RUPA § 202(a). Under UPA § 13, RUPA § 305(a), the partnership is liable for loss or injury caused to a person as a result of a wrongful act or omission of a partner acting in the ordinary course of business of the partnership or with authority of the partnership. Lisa committed a tort ("negligence") when she negligently bumped into Mark and caused him to fall. This tort constitutes a wrongful act, and Lisa was acting in the ordinary course of business of the partnership. Hence, the partnership is liable to Mark. At this point, a note on the terminology is in order. Under the Revised Uniform Partnership act, the partnership is a legal entity distinct from its partners, RUPA § 201, and can therefore be liable. Under the old UPA, the partnership is nothing else but the partners as a group. However, even under the old UPA, we say that the partnership is liable, cf. § 13 UPA.

Lisa, Mary, and Nora are jointly and severally liable for the $100. This is because under UPA § 15(a), RUPA § 306(a), all partners are jointly and severally liable for the partnership's tort liabilities.

But how about Alma? Under UPA § 17, RUPA § 306, a partner is not personally liable for partnership obligations that arose before the partner joined the partnership. In other words, new partners are not liable for old debts. Alma joined the partnership on January 18, 2013, and hence after the partnership had incurred the obligation to Mark (which happened on January 17, 2013). Therefore, Alma is not liable to Mark.

(A) is incorrect.

See the answer to choice D.

(B) is incorrect.

See the answer to choice D.

(C) is incorrect.

See the answer to choice D.

Answer to Question 24

(B) is the correct answer.

Note, first, that on January 1, 2013, Richard, Clive, and Owen formed a partnership, because they created an association of two or more persons to carry on a business as co-owners for profit (cf. RUPA § 202(a)).

Under the RUPA, the death of a partner does not dissolve the partnership if at least two other partners remain; rather, the partner's death will only cause that partner's dissociation from the partnership under RUPA § 601(7)(i). Under the old UPA (1914), the death of any partner will dissolve the partnership under UPA § 31(4). Given that this partnership was governed by the RUPA, Richard's death did not dissolve it.

What about Clive's death. As noted above, a partner's death does not generally dissolve a partnership under the RUPA. However, in this particular case, there is an additional factor to consider: as a result of Clive's death, only one of the partners remains. This is crucial, because by definition, a partnership requires two or more persons (cf. UPA § 6(1), RUPA § 202(a)). Therefore, even though RUPA § 801 does not mention the death of a partner as a ground for dissolution, those courts that have addressed the issue have generally held that the death of one partner in a two-person partnership leads to the partnership's dissolution. Therefore, the partnership was dissolved on the day that Clive died, i.e., on January 5, 2013.

(A) is incorrect.

See the answer to choice B.

(C) is incorrect.

See the answer to choice B.

(D) is incorrect.

See the answer to choice B.

Answer to Question 25

(D) is the correct answer.

Note, first, that Pamela and Joe were partners, because they had formed an association of two or more persons to carry on a business as co-owners for profit (cf. RUPA § 202(a)). According to RUPA § 306, all partners are jointly and severally liable for the debts of a partnership. The question, though, is whether Pamela's purchase of the violins has created a partnership debt. For a partner to bind the partnership to a contract, two conditions must generally be satisfied. First, the partner must have acted on behalf of the partnership. Since Pamela explicitly acted in the name of the store, this requirement is met. Second, the partner must have had the power to bind the partnership.

To determine whether a partner has the power to bind the partnership, one has to distinguish. If the partner acts with authority, then the acting partner always has the power to bind the partnership (cf. RUPA § 301; UPA § 9). However, note that the term "with authority" has a special meaning in partnership law: One must look at the internal division of power between the partners. If internally (i.e., as between the partners) the partner was allowed to act for the partnership, then she acted with authority and therefore, externally, she had the power to bind the partnership.

So how does one know whether the partner was allowed to act according to the internal division of power? That question is answered by RUPA § 401(j) (or UPA § 18(h)), and the relevant rules can be summarized as follows:

First, one has to look to the partnership agreement. The partnership agreement can only be amended with the consent of all the partners, so if the partnership agreement stipulates what the partners may or may not do, the relevant provision is binding unless all of the partners agree otherwise.

If the partnership agreement is silent, then the following rules apply: Any act *outside the ordinary course of business* can only be undertaken if all the partners consent. This rule is expressly contained in RUPA § 401(j), but it also applies under the UPA (1914). With respect to acts *within the ordinary course of business* of the partnership, one has to distinguish. In principle, any partner is allowed to undertake them. However, one important restriction applies: Any difference of opinion between the partners can be decided by a majority of the partners (UPA § 18(h) and RUPA § 401(j).) This decision is then binding even on the partner who did not consent.

In the case at hand, Pamela and Joe had come to an agreement that Pamela could only purchase soccer balls for the store. As a general rule, a partnership agreement does not have to be in writing. Rather, oral agreements between the partners are binding as well. Of course, partnership agreements remain subject to the general Statute of Frauds. Hence, an oral partnership agreement is unenforceable if it is for a term of more than one year. However, a so-called at-will partnership—that is, a partnership that has been entered into for an indefinite time and can be terminated at any time by any partner— is generally thought to be capable of being performed within one year and therefore does not fall within the one-year rule of the Statute of Frauds. In the case at hand, the Statute of Frauds does not apply, and the partners' agreement regarding the extent of Pamela's authority is binding. Accordingly, Pamela did not have authority to purchase the violins.

However, Pamela's lack of authority does not necessarily imply that she lacked the power to bind the partnership. Rather, if the acting partner lacked authority for the transaction that he has undertaken, one has to distinguish between those acts that appear to be for the carrying on of the partnership business in the usual way and those acts that do not fall into this category.

If the act *does not* appear to be for the carrying on of the partnership business in the usual way, then the partnership will not be bound by a partner acting without authority (RUPA § 301(2)). By contrast, If the act appears to be for the carrying on of the partnership business in the usual way, then the general principle is that the partnership will be bound by the act, even though the acting partner acted without authority (RUPA § 301(1)). However, the partnership is not bound if the third party knew or had received notification that the partner lacked authority (RUPA § 301(1)). In the case at hand, the partnership's business was a soccer equipment store, and so purchasing violins was not in the ordinary course of the partnership's business.

Even so, our analysis is not quite finished. That is because the RUPA introduces an additional layer of protection for third parties in the form of the rules governing the statement of partnership authority. As a general matter, a grant of authority contained in such a statement is conclusive in favor of the third party, RUPA § 303(d)(1). However, this protection is subject to various restrictions. In particular, the statement can be canceled, and, even if it has not been canceled by the partnership, it is canceled automatically five years after the most recent amendment, RUPA § 303(g). In the case at hand, the statement of partnership authority was filed in year 2000, and there is no indication that it has been amended since. Accordingly, it was canceled in 2005 and thus could not protect Robert when he sold the violins in 2010. It follows that the sale of the violins did not create a partnership liability. Therefore, Joe is not personally liable with respect to the $1,500,000.

(A) is incorrect.

Joe is not liable. See the answer to choice D.

(B) is incorrect.

Joe is not liable. See the answer to choice D.

(C) is incorrect.

This answer contains an incorrect statement of law. As a general rule, the statement of partnership authority generally cannot be invoked against *third parties*, RUPA § 303(f). An exception can be found in RUPA § 303. Under that provision, "a person not a partner is deemed to know of a limitation on the authority of a partner to transfer real property held in the name of the partnership if a certified copy of the filed statement containing the limitation on authority is of record in the office for recording transfers of that real property." By contrast, the statement of partnership authority typically *can* be invoked against the partnership, § 303(d).

CHAPTER 7
CORPORATE LAW

Answer to Question 1

(D) is the correct answer.

According to DGCL § 102(a)(2), the certificate of incorporation has to name the address of the corporation's registered office in Delaware. Furthermore, DGCL § 102(a)(3) provides that the certificate of incorporation has to contain the nature of the business or purposes to be conducted or promoted. Admittedly, it is sufficient to state that the purpose of the corporation is to engage in any lawful act or activity for which corporations may be organized under the General Corporation Law of Delaware, DGCL § 102(a)(3). However, the fact that the purpose can be of a very general nature does not eliminate the necessity to state this purpose in the certificate of incorporation. Moreover, according to DGCL § 102(a)(5), the certificate of incorporation must include the name and mailing address of the incorporator or incorporators.

(A) is incorrect.

See the answer to choice D.

(B) is incorrect.

See the answer to choice D.

(C) is incorrect.

See the answer to choice D.

Answer to Question 2

(A) is the correct answer.

The dissolution of the corporation in case of deadlock is governed by DGCL § 273. Under that provision, the Delaware Chancery Court can dissolve a corporation with two shareholders, each of whom owns 50%, if one of the shareholders petitions for the corporation's dissolution and if the shareholders are "unable to agree upon the desirability of discontinuing such joint venture and disposing of the assets used in such venture." These conditions are met in the case at hand.

(B) is incorrect.

See the answer to choice A.

(C) is incorrect.

See the answer to choice A.

(D) is incorrect.

See the answer to choice A.

Answer to Question 3

(A) is the correct answer.

Under Delaware law, the duty of loyalty requires the directors to act in the best interest of the corporation. However, this does not mean that the directors have to bow to the wishes of the shareholders. Rather, as the Court of Chancery explained in *American Int'l. Rent a Car, Inc. v. Cross* (1984 Del. Ch. LEXIS 413 (Del. Ch. 1984)), it is not "a per se breach of fiduciary duty for the Board to act in a manner which it may believe is contrary to the wishes of a majority of the company's stockholders." Rather, the directors must act according to what *they* believe is the in best interest of the corporation, even if the shareholders disagree. Since Rudy believed the move to the new office to be in the corporation's best interest, he has not breached his duty of loyalty.

Moreover, Rudy has not breached his duty of care either. A violation of the duty of care occurs where a director acts without being reasonably informed. The burden of proof is on the plaintiff. In the case at hand, Rudy made his decision only after carefully investigating and analyzing all relevant facts. (The facts mention that "the board" investigated and analyzed all relevant facts, but the corporation only has a single director, namely Rudy.) Accordingly, Rudy did not violate his duty of care.

(B) is incorrect.

See the answer to choice A.

(C) is incorrect.

See the answer to choice A.

(D) is incorrect.

See the answer to choice A.

Answer to Question 4

(C) is the correct answer.

DGCL § 102(b)(7) allows provisions eliminating the liability of corporate directors for fiduciary duty violations. However, "such provision shall not eliminate or limit the liability of a director . . . [f]or any breach of the director's duty of loyalty to the corporation or its stockholders." Accordingly, any provision seeking to limit or eliminate the liability of a director to the corporation or its stockholders for monetary damages for breach of the duty of loyalty violates Delaware law.

(A) is incorrect.

According to DGCL § 102(b)(5), the certificate of incorporation may contain a "provision limiting the duration of the corporation's existence to a specified date."

(B) is incorrect.

Under DGCL § 102(b)(6), the certificate of incorporation may contain "[a] provision imposing personal liability for the debts of the corporation on its stockholders."

(D) is incorrect.

Under DGCL § 102(b)(4), the certificate of incorporation may contain "[p]rovisions requiring for any corporate action, the vote of a larger portion of the stock or of any class or series thereof, or of any other securities having voting power, or a larger number of the directors, than is required by this chapter." The term "this chapter" refers to the Delaware General Corporation Law.

Answer to Question 5

(D) is the correct answer.

To solve this question correctly, it is essential to understand the difference between a corporation's net assets and its capital. A corporation's net assets equal its total assets minus its total liabilities, DGCL § 154. In the case at hand, the facts explicitly state that the corporation's net assets amount to $10,000,000.

A corporation's capital is an entirely different concept and one that can best be understood in the context of the rules governing dividends: As a general rule, corporations cannot distribute all of their assets to their shareholders as dividends. Rather, they can only pay dividends "out of [their] surplus," DGCL § 170(a), or, in the absence of a surplus, out of their "net profits for the fiscal year in which the dividend is declared and/or the preceding fiscal year."

Let us ignore, for now, the rule that dividends can be declared out of the profits for the current or the preceding fiscal year. Then corporations can only declare dividends out of their surplus. The surplus is defined as the amount by which the corporation's net assets exceed its capital, DGCL § 154. Thus, the term "capital" refers to the amount that the corporation has to hold in reserve before it can pay dividends. In other words, the law wants corporations to amass a "financial safety cushion" before they can distribute money to their stockholders, and the corporation's "capital" is the number that tells us how big that financial safety cushion must be.

It is crucial to understand this difference between net assets and legal capital. The term "net assets" refers to the assets that the corporation *actually has*. By contrast, the term "capital" refers to the amount of assets that the corporation *must have* before it can pay dividends. For example, if the corporation has $1,300,000 in assets and a capital of $1,000,000, then the corporation can pay $300,000 in dividends.

Note that a corporation's capital tells you very little about the corporation's actual assets. For example, assume that a corporation's capital is $10,000. Does that mean that the corporation has net assets in the amount of $10,000? Absolutely not. Rather, a capital of $10,000 only means that unless the corporation has assets in excess of $10,000 (or has made profits in the current or preceding fiscal year), the corporation cannot pay any dividends. But the corporation's assets may in fact be much lower (or higher) than the corporation's capital. For example, despite having a capital of $10,000, the corporation may only have assets in the amount of $2000.

Does a corporation violate the law if its assets are less than its capital? Not necessarily. Assume, for example, that a corporation's capital is $10,000. Furthermore, assume that the corporation has net assets in the amount of $11,000, but that the corporation has not made any profit for five years. If the corporation now pays a dividend in the aggregate amount of $2000 and thereby lowers its net assets to $9000, then the corporation violates Delaware law. That is because the corporation's surplus (net assets minus capital) was only $1000, and in the absence of profits, the corporation was only allowed to pay dividends out of its surplus. By contrast, if the corporation's net assets are reduced from $11,000 to $9000 because the corporation's business loses money or because the corporation's warehouse is hit by lightning, no violation of Delaware law occurs. In other words, the law does not impose a duty on corporations to have net assets in the amount of the corporation's capital. Rather, the law simply provides that a corporation *cannot pay dividends* unless its net assets exceeds its capital (or unless the corporation has made profits in the current or the preceding fiscal year).

So how high was the corporation's capital in the case at hand? Crucially, a corporation's capital is not necessarily constant, but can—and typically will—change over time. Hence, you need to proceed in chronological order: You start with the last known capital, and then you look for anything that might have increased or decreased the corporation's capital.

Newly upon formation, the capital of the corporation was zero. This changed when the corporation issued the par value shares. Under DGCL § 154, the default rule is that when a corporation issues par value shares, the capital is increased by the aggregate par value of the relevant shares. Because Hypo Corp. made no resolution regarding the effect of the share issuance on the corporation's capital, we can apply the legal default. This means that the corporation's capital was increased by ten times ten dollars, i.e., by $100.

On June 1, 2015, the corporation issued the no-par value shares. Under § 154 of the Delaware General Corporation Law, the default rule is that when a corporation issues no-par value shares, the capital is increased by the total consideration received for those shares. In the case at hand, the board made no resolution regarding the impact of the share issuance on the corporation's capital, and we can therefore apply the default. This means that the corporation's capital was increased by an amount equal to the whole consideration, i.e. $200 (10 x $20). Thus, following the share issuance on June 1, 2013, the corporation's capital was $100 + $200 = $300.

On August 1, 2015, the board adopted a resolution to increase the capital. According to DGCL § 154 of the Delaware General Corporation Law, the board can only increase the capital via a board resolution if, after the increase, the net assets are still greater than the capital. In the case at hand, that requirement is met: After the resolution, the capital amounted to $100 + $200

+ \$50,000 = \$50,300. At the same time, the net assets amounted to \$10,000,000. Given that the resolution was valid, the capital is now \$50,300.

(A) is incorrect.

See the answer to choice D.

(B) is incorrect.

See the answer to choice D.

(C) is incorrect.

See the answer to choice D.

Answer to Question 6

(D) is the correct answer.

Under DGCL § 154, the directors may at any time increase the corporation's capital by a board resolution "directing that a portion of the net assets of the corporation in excess of" the corporation's capital "be transferred to the capital account." Therefore, you first need to calculate the net assets. According to DGCL § 154 of the Delaware General Corporation Law, "net assets means the amount by which total assets exceed total liabilities." In other words, net assets equal total assets minus total liabilities (i.e. \$22,000 − \$5,000 = \$17,000). Because the capital can be increased by "a portion of the net assets of the corporation in excess of the corporation's capital," DGCL § 154, we then have to determine the amount by which the net assets exceed the capital, which amounts to net assets minus capital (i.e. \$17,000 − \$10,000 = \$7,000). Therefore, the board could only increase the capital by a portion of \$7,000, which means that choices A, B, and C are incorrect.

(A) is incorrect.

See the answer to choice D.

(B) is incorrect.

See the answer to choice D.

(C) is incorrect.

See the answer to choice D.

Answer to Question 7

(A) is the correct answer.

According to DGCL § 131(a), the corporation's registered office has to be located in Delaware.

(B) is incorrect.

DGCL § 131(a) explicitly provides that the corporation's registered office does not have to be the same as its place of business. In fact, it is absolutely standard for corporations to have their place of business in some other state such as Texas or Illinois while having merely a registered office in Delaware. Moreover, the registered office requirement is typically satisfied with the help of a service company that serves as a registered agent for thousands of companies. The result is that for thousands of companies, the registered office can be found at the same address, namely at the address of the relevant service provider.

(C) is incorrect.

The Delaware General Corporation Law contains no requirement that the corporation's registered office must be located at the address of one of the incorporators.

(D) is incorrect.

See the answer to choice A.

Answer to Question 8

(A) is the correct answer.

The number of directors does not have to be fixed in the certificate of incorporation. In particular, it can also be fixed in the bylaws, DGCL § 141(b).

(B) is incorrect.

A director may in fact resign at any time, DGCL § 141(b).

(C) is incorrect.

It is true that "[d]irectors need not be stockholders unless so required by the certificate of incorporation or the bylaws," DGCL § 141(b).

(D) is incorrect.

See the answer to choice A.

Answer to Question 9

(D) is the correct answer.

Under DGCL § 174 of the Delaware General Corporation Law, a corporation may pay dividends either out of its surplus—this is the so-called *surplus rule*—or, in case there is no surplus, out of "its net profits for the fiscal year in which the dividend is declared and/or the preceding fiscal year"—this is known as the *nimble dividends rule*.

According to DGCL § 154 of the Delaware General Corporation Law, the surplus equals the "excess, if any, at any given time, of the net assets of the corporation over the amount so determined to be capital shall be surplus." Furthermore, the net assets refer to "the amount by which total assets exceed total liabilities." In the case at hand, the net assets equal $1,000,000 and so does the legal capital, so that the corporation does not have any surplus. Accordingly, the desired dividend cannot be paid out of the surplus.

Under the nimble dividends rule, a corporation that has no surplus may pay a dividend out of "its net profits for the fiscal year in which the dividend is declared and/or the preceding fiscal year." However, in the case at hand, the corporation has not made a profit for the last five years, and therefore cannot invoke the nimble dividends rule either. It follows that it would be illegal for the corporation to pay a dividend at this time.

(A) is incorrect.

See the answer to choice D.

(B) is incorrect.

See the answer to choice D.

(C) is incorrect.

See the answer to choice D.

Answer to Question 10

(B) is the correct answer.

Under DGCL § 141(k) of the Delaware General Corporation Law, the general rule is that "[a]ny director may be removed with or without cause, by the holders of a majority of the shares then entitled to vote at an election of directors." Hence, unless the corporation has a classified board, the removal of directors does not require cause.

But can the shareholders make their voice heard? It is not possible for the shareholders to call a special meeting. Under DGCL § 211(d), special shareholder meetings may only be called "by the board of directors or by such person or persons as may be authorized by the certificate of incorporation or by the bylaws." In the case at hand, the corporation's certificate of incorporation and bylaws do not enable anyone to call special meetings.

However, under DGCL § 228(b), shareholders can take action without an annual meeting and even without a vote "if a consent or consents in writing, setting forth the action so taken, shall be signed by the holders of outstanding stock having not less than the minimum number of votes that would be necessary to authorize or take such action at a meeting at which all shares entitled to vote thereon were present and voted . . ." In other words, George can be removed by written consent as long as the consent is signed by the holders of a majority of the outstanding shares entitled to vote in an election of directors.

(A) is incorrect.

Under DGCL § 211(d), the shareholders do not have the right to insist on a special meeting. See the answer to choice B.

(C) is incorrect.

Under DGCL § 141(k), the general rule is that "[a]ny director may be removed with or without cause, by the holders of a majority of the shares then entitled to vote at an election of directors." See the answer to choice B.

(D) is incorrect.

George can be removed by written consent under DGCL § 228(b). See the answer to choice B.

Answer to Question 11

(D) is the correct answer.

See the answers to choices A, B, and C.

(A) is incorrect.

Whereas a majority of all public corporations in the United States are incorporated in Delaware, most closely held corporations—which constitute the vast majority of all corporations—are incorporated locally, i.e. in the state where their primary place of business is located.

(B) is incorrect.

In a merger, two or more corporations are combined in such a way that only one of them still continues to exist after the merger, DGCL § 251(a). The law refers to the latter corporation as the "surviving corporation," DGCL § 251(b)(3). When two corporations combine and the result is a wholly new corporation formed as part of the transaction, the law uses the term "consolidation," DGCL § 251(a).

(C) is incorrect.

In a short-form merger, approval by the shareholders of the parent corporation is always necessary when the subsidiary corporation is the surviving corporation, DGCL § 253(a).

Answer to Question 12

(D) is the correct answer.

According to DGCL § 141(b), the legal default is that a "majority of the total number of directors shall constitute a quorum for the transaction of business."

(A) is incorrect.

According to DGCL § 141(g), the legal default is that board meetings may be held outside of Delaware.

(B) is incorrect.

According to DGCL § 141(h), the legal default is that "the board of directors shall have the authority to fix the compensation of directors."

(C) is incorrect.

When the board of directors consists of two or three classes of directors, we say that the board is "classified." According to DGCL § 141(d), the legal default is boards are not classified. Of course, in practice, classified boards are by no means unusual. In particular, among IPO firms (firms that have an initial public offering), the vast majority have classified boards.

Answer to Question 13

(C) is the correct answer.

In a limited partnership, there are two types of partners, namely limited partners and general partners. While the limited partners are not personally liable for debts of the partnership beyond any contribution that they have promised, any general partner faces unlimited personal liability. Moreover, each limited partnership must have at least one general partner. Therefore, the limited partnership does not offer the benefit of limited liability to all of its owners.

(A) is incorrect.

As a general rule, the shareholders of a corporation are not liable for the corporation's debts unless the certificate of incorporation provides otherwise.

(B) is incorrect.

According to the legal default, the members of a limited liability company are not liable for the limited liability company's debts.

(D) is incorrect.

As a general rule, the shareholders of a statutory corporation are not liable for the statutory close corporation's debts unless the certificate of incorporation provides otherwise.

Answer to Question 14

(A) is the correct answer.

The internal affairs of a corporation are governed by the law of the state where the corporation has been incorporated. Since Gold Corp. was incorporated in Delaware, it is governed by Delaware Law.

Admittedly, New York and California have adopted so-called "pseudo-foreign corporation statutes" that apply parts of New York and California corporate law to corporations that have been formed elsewhere, but have strong business contacts to New York and California (cf. Cal. Corp. Code § 2115, N.Y. Bus. Corp. L. §§ 1317–1320). However, these pseudo-foreign corporation statutes do not apply to publicly traded corporations, and Gold Corp. is a publicly traded corporation. Moreover, in the case at hand, Gold Corp. does not have any contacts to California or New York.

(B) is incorrect.

See the answer to choice A.

(C) is incorrect.

See the answer to choice A.

(D) is incorrect.

See the answer to choice A.

Answer to Question 15

(D) is the correct answer.

Originally, the corporation's capital was zero. That changed when the corporation issued the no-par value shares on January 1, 2014. With no-par value shares, the default rule enshrined in DGCL § 154 is that the capital is increased by an amount corresponding to the total consideration received for the no-par value shares. The board can decide to deviate from that default by board resolution, DGCL § 154, but if the shares are issued for cash, that resolution has to be adopted by the time the shares are issued. Here, the total consideration received for the no-par value shares was 10 times $1,000, and so amounted to $10,000. To be sure, the board did adopt a resolution according to which only part of the consideration received for the no-par value shares should be capital, but that resolution came too late. Hence, as a result of issuing the no-par value shares, the capital of the corporation was increased from $0 to $10,000.

The board later tried to lower the capital on January 18, 2014. In principle, a reduction of capital is possible, DGCL § 154. However, under DGCL § 244(b), no such reduction is possible if, after the reduction, the corporation's assets are insufficient to pay its debts. That, of course, is the case here. Even before the intended reduction, the total liabilities were greater than the corporation's total assets, and that would not have changed as a result of the reduction in capital. Hence, after the board meeting on January 18, 2014, the capital is $10,000.

(A) is incorrect.

See the answer to choice D.

(B) is incorrect.

See the answer to choice D.

(C) is incorrect.

See the answer to choice D.

Answer to Question 16

(A) is the correct answer.

The crucial provision to answer this question is DGCL § 160(c). Its wording is a bit complicated, but the underlying idea is quite simple. The law does not want directors of a given corporation to use shares owned by that corporation to secure their own reelection. For example, imagine that you are the director of Spring Corp. and you are trying to get reelected. Without DGCL § 160(c), you could simply let Spring Corp. acquire a majority of its own shares, and at the next annual meeting, you could—acting in Spring Corp.'s name— vote these shares in favor of your own reelection. That is why DGCL § 160(c) prohibits the corporation from voting its own shares.

Of course, if you are a Spring Corp. director trying to secure your own reelection, you may take a somewhat more sophisticated approach. For example, you could let Spring Corp. acquire, directly or indirectly, a majority of the shares of Fall Corp. and then use these shares to elect your cronies to the board of Fall Corp. Now that you control the board of Fall Corp., you could ensure that Fall Corp. buys a sizeable number of your own company's (Spring Corp.'s) shares and votes them in your favor at Spring Corp.'s next annual meeting. To prevent such a scheme, DGCL § 160(c) also prohibits those shares from being voted that are indirectly controlled by the corporation where the vote takes place. Keeping these principles in mind, let us to turn to the text of DGCL § 160(c) which reads as follows:

Shares of its own capital stock belonging to the corporation or to another corporation, if a majority of the shares entitled to vote in the election of directors of such other corporation is held, directly or indirectly, by the corporation, shall neither be entitled to vote nor be counted for quorum purposes.

The term "the corporation" refers to the corporation where the shareholder meeting, i.e., the vote, takes place. In other words, in our case, "the corporation" is Spring Corp. Furthermore, the phrase "own capital stock" refers to shares issued by "the corporation." In other words, the "shares of its own capital stock" are the shares that you need to elect the directors of "the corporation." Thus, in our case, you can read DGCL § 160(c) as follows:

> [Spring Corp. shares] belonging to [Spring Corp.] or to another corporation, if a majority of the shares entitled to vote in the election of directors of such other corporation is held, directly or indirectly, by [Spring Corp.], shall neither be entitled to vote nor be counted for quorum purposes.

The term "other corporation" refers to any corporation that holds shares in the corporation where the shareholder meeting takes place. In other words, if X-corporation holds shares in Y corporation, and Y corporation wants to know whether the shares held by X corporation can be counted at Y corporation's annual meeting, then Y corporation is "the corporation" (because that is where the annual meeting/the vote takes place) and X-corporation is the "other corporation" (because X-corporation owns the shares that we are trying to throw out). Thus, in our case, you can read DGCL § 160(c) as follows:

> [Spring Corp. shares] belonging to [Spring Corp.] or to [Fall Corp.], if a majority of the shares entitled to vote in the election of directors of [Fall Corp.] is held, directly or indirectly, by [Spring Corp.], shall neither be entitled to vote nor be counted for quorum purposes.

So in other words, you cannot count Spring Corp. shares belonging to Fall Corp. if a majority of the shares entitled to vote in the election of directors of Fall Corp. is held directly or indirectly by Spring Corp. So the question is: Does Spring Corp., directly or indirectly hold a majority of the shares entitled to vote in the election of directors of Fall Corp.?

Admittedly, Spring Corp. does not *directly* hold a majority of the shares entitled to vote in the election of directors Fall Corp. After all, Spring Corp. does not hold any Fall Corp. stock. But Spring Corp. holds *indirectly* a majority of the shares entitled to vote in the election of directors of Fall Corp. That is because Spring Corp. holds a majority of Summer Corp. stock and Summer Corp. holds a majority of the common stock of Fall Corp. It follows that under DGCL § 160(c), the shares held by Fall Corp. cannot be voted or counted for quorum purposes at the annual meeting of Spring Corp.

(B) is incorrect.

See the answer to choice A.

(C) is incorrect.

See the answer to choice A.

(D) is incorrect.

See the answer to choice A.

Answer to Question 17

(D) is the correct answer.

Section 160(c) of the Delaware General Corporation Law reads as follows:

Shares of its own capital stock belonging to the corporation or to another corporation, if a majority of the shares entitled to vote in the election of directors of such other corporation is held, directly or indirectly, by the corporation, shall neither be entitled to vote nor be counted for quorum purposes.

The term "the corporation" refers to the corporation where the shareholder meeting and hence the vote takes place. In other words, in our case, "the corporation" is Monday Corp. Furthermore, the term "own capital stock" refers to shares issued by "the corporation." In other words, the "shares of its own capital stock" are the shares that you need to elect the directors of "the corporation." Thus, in our case, you can read DGCL § 160(c) as follows:

[Monday Corp. shares] belonging to [Monday Corp.] or to another corporation, if a majority of the shares entitled to vote in the election of directors of such other corporation is held, directly or indirectly, by [Monday Corp.], shall neither be entitled to vote nor be counted for quorum purposes.

The term "other corporation" refers to any corporation that holds shares in the corporation where the annual meeting takes place. In other words, if X corporation holds shares in Y corporation, and Y corporation wants to know if these shares can be counted at Y corporation's annual meeting, then Y corporation is "the corporation" [because that is where the annual meeting takes place) and X-corporation is the "other corporation" (because X-corporation owns the shares that we are trying to throw out). Thus, in our case, you can read DGCL § 160(c) as follows:

[Monday Corp. shares] belonging to [Monday Corp.] or to [Wednesday Corp.], if a majority of the shares entitled to vote in the election of directors of [Wednesday Corp.] is held, directly or indirectly, by [Monday Corp.], shall neither be entitled to vote nor be counted for quorum purposes.

So in other words, you cannot count Monday Corp. shares belonging to Wednesday Corp. if a majority of the shares entitled to vote in the election of directors of Wednesday Corp. is held directly or indirectly by Monday Corp. The question is then, does Monday Corp. hold a majority of the shares entitled to vote in the election of directors Wednesday Corp., either directly or indirectly?

Monday Corp. does not "directly" hold a majority of the shares entitled to vote in the election of directors Wednesday Corp. After all, Monday Corp. does not hold any Wednesday Corp. stock. Moreover, Monday Corp. does not *indirectly* hold a majority of the shares entitled to vote in the election of directors of Wednesday Corp. either. That is because Tuesday Corp. only holds one percent of the shares of Wednesday Corp. That is not enough to give Tuesday Corp. control of Wednesday Corp., and therefore we cannot the shares held by Wednesday Corp. as though they were held by Monday Corp. It follows that DGCL § 160(c) of the Delaware General Corporation Law does not apply. Accordingly, the shares held by Wednesday Corp. can be voted and counted for quorum purposes at the annual meeting of Monday Corp. Note that this makes a lot of sense. Given that Tuesday Corp. holds only one percent of the shares of Wednesday Corp., Tuesday Corp. has no control over how Wednesday Corp. will vote its shares, and accordingly, Monday Corp. also lacks control over how Wednesday Corp. will vote its shares. Hence, there is no danger that by allowing Wednesday Corp. to vote its shares at the annual shareholder meeting of Monday Corp., Monday Corp. will somehow control the outcome of that election.

(A) is incorrect.

See the answer to choice D.

(B) is incorrect.

See the answer to choice D.

(C) is incorrect.

See the answer to choice D.

Answer to Question 18

(A) is the correct answer.

There is an easy and well-known formula to solve this question. The number of shares held by the shareholder must be greater than $(C \times S) / (D + 1)$, where C is the number of candidates that the shareholder wants to get elected to the board, S is the total number of shares, and D is the number of directorships to be filled.

In the case at hand, there are three directors to be elected, so $D = 3$. The total number of outstanding shares is 10, so $S = 10$. In order to be sure that she can elect one of her candidates, the number of shares held by Julia must be greater than $(1 \times 10) / (3 + 1) = 10 / 4$. Here, Julia holds 3 shares (which amounts to $12 / 4$) so she has enough shares to secure the election of one of her candidates.

By contrast, to elect two of her candidates, the number of shares held by Julia would have to be greater than $(2 \times 10) / (3 + 1) = 5$. But Julia holds only 3 shares and therefore cannot be sure that more than one of her candidates will be elected.

(B) is incorrect.

See the answer to choice A.

(C) is incorrect.

See the answer to choice A.

(D) is incorrect.

See the answer to choice A.

Answer to Question 19

(A) is the correct answer.

Morse can expect to be elected, and here is why. As a general matter, a "majority of the shares entitled to vote, present in person or represented by proxy constitute a quorum at a meeting of stockholders," DGCL § 216(1). Furthermore, a director needs a plurality of the vote to be elected, DGCL § 216(3). In the case at hand, the overall of number of shares represented at the shareholder meeting of Lewis Corp. is 70, since the only shares present or represented by proxy are the 40 shares held by Edward Corp. and the 30 shares held by Phil.

Obviously, if the 40 shares held by Edward Corp. can be voted and counted for quorum purposes, then the quorum requirement is satisfied, since 70 out of 100 shares are represented by proxy. Moreover, in that case, the 40 shares that will be voted in favor of Morse will be sufficient to give Morse a plurality of the vote, since the other candidate, Kit, only stands to receive 30 votes.

The question, then, is whether the 40 shares held by Edward Corp. can be voted and counted for quorum purposes. A possible obstacle is DGCL § 160(c). Under that provision, the shares held by Edward Corp. cannot be voted or counted for quorum purposes if they "belong" to Lewis Corp. or if they are held by a 50+% subsidiary of Lewis Corp.

In the case at hand, the shares held by Edward Corp. did not formally belong to Lewis Corp. (They were, after all, held by Edward Corp.) Now the term "belong" to can sometimes be interpreted more generously if the circumstances are sufficiently unusual (see *Speiser v. Baker*, 525 A2d 1001 (Del. Ch. 1987)). However, in the case at hand, there is no indication that the situation is sufficiently atypical to justify an expansive application of DGCL § 160(c).

Thus, the question remains whether the shares held by Edward Corp. are held by a corporation that is a direct or indirect 50% subsidiary of Lewis Corp. That, however, is not the case. To be sure, Lewis Corp. owns more than 60% of Vivian Corp.'s voting stock. Hence, Vivian Corp. is controlled by Lewis Corp. However, Vivian Corp. only owns 5 shares of Edward Corp. It follows that Edward Corp. can vote the shares it holds in Lewis Corp. Therefore, Morse has enough votes to be elected regardless of whether the certificate calls for cumulative voting or regular voting.

(B) is incorrect.

See the answer to choice A.

(C) is incorrect.

See the answer to choice A.

(D) is incorrect.

See the answer to choice A.

Answer to Question 20

(A) is the correct answer.

Let us start with the question of whether Rich can hold Carla and Thrifty Corp. liable. Carla and Thrifty Corp. have created a partnership to run the restaurant, since they have formed an association of two or more persons to carry on as co-owners a business for profit, UPA § 6, RUPA § 202(a).

Is the loan a partnership liability? A contract entered into by one of the partners binds the partnership if the partner acts on behalf of the partnership and with the power to bind the partnership. When Tim obtained, the loan, he made it clear that he was representing Thrifty Corp. and that Thrifty Corp. in turn was acting on behalf of the restaurant, i.e. the partnership.

Did Tim have the power to bind the partnership? As UPA § 9, RUPA § 306 make clear, a partner has the power to bind the partnership if he acts with authority, though he can sometimes bind the partnership even if he lacks authority. A partner acts with authority if his actions are authorized by the partnership agreement, if the other partners have agreed to his actions, or, failing that, if his actions are undertaken within the ordinary course of business. In the case at hand, Carla had given her consent to obtaining the loan. Therefore, Tim acted with authority and thus had the power to bind the partnership. It follows that the loan agreement has created a partnership liability. Under UPA § 15, RUPA § 306, the partners are personally liable for the debts of the partnership.

Can Rich also hold Tim personally liable? This would be the case if Tim could be held liable for the liability for Thrifty Corp., since, as noted above, Thrifty Corp. is liable to Rich. Generally, shareholders are not personally liable for the debts of the corporation, DGCL § 102(b)(6). However, courts will sometimes pierce the corporate veil. In the case at hand, not only is the corporation undercapitalized, but, more importantly, Tim has resorted to a deliberate misrepresentation regarding the corporation's assets. Since courts generally pierce the veil in case of fraud, these factors are sufficient to justify veil-piercing. Hence, Tim will be held personally liable.

(B) is incorrect.

See the answer to choice A.

(C) is incorrect.

See the answer to choice A.

(D) is incorrect.

See the answer to choice A.

Answer to Question 21

(A) is the correct answer.

The bylaw classifying the board is in fact void. According to DGCL § 141(d), the board can be classified, but only "by the certificate of incorporation or by an initial bylaw, or by a bylaw adopted by a vote of the stockholders." In the case at hand, the bylaw was neither adopted by the stockholders, nor did it constitute an initial bylaw. Therefore, the bylaw could not classify the board.

(B) is incorrect.

The bylaw is void. See the answer to choice A.

(C) is incorrect.

The bylaw is void. See the answer to choice A.

(D) is incorrect.

The bylaw is void. See the answer to choice A.

Answer to Question 22

(B) is the correct answer.

Under the legal default, the corporation's shareholders have the power to adopt, amend, or repeal bylaws, DGCL § 109(a). To be sure, the "corporation may, in its certificate of incorporation, confer the power to adopt, amend or repeal bylaws upon the directors," DGCL § 109(a), and Gold Corp. has made use of that option. However, even then, DGCL § 109(a) makes it clear that "[t]he fact that such power has been so conferred upon the directors . . . shall not divest the stockholders . . . of the power, nor limit their power to adopt, amend or repeal bylaws." In other words, even where—as in the present case— the certificate of incorporation empowers the board to adopt, amend, or repeal bylaws, the shareholders still retain their power to adopt, amend, or repeal bylaws as well.

Moreover, according to the legal default, "[a] majority of the shares entitled to vote, present in person or represented by proxy, shall constitute a quorum at a meeting of stockholders," DGCL § 216(1). Furthermore, "[i]n all matters other than the election of directors, the affirmative vote of the majority of shares present in person or represented by proxy at the meeting and entitled to vote on the subject matter shall be the act of the stockholders," DGCL § 216(2). In other words, a simple majority of the outstanding shares entitled to vote is needed for the quorum, and a simple majority of the shares present or represented at the shareholder meeting is needed for decision at the shareholder meeting. In the case at hand, both requirements are met.

However, under DGCL § 109(2), bylaw provisions must not be "inconsistent with law." The term "law" includes the provisions of the Delaware General Corporation Law and, in particular, DGCL § 141(a) according to which "[t]he business and affairs of every corporation . . . shall be managed by or under the direction of a board of directors." Deciding whether or not to adopt a poison pill is part of managing the corporation and is thus a responsibility that DGCL § 141(a) reserves for the board. The bylaw at issue interferes with the board's responsibility and thereby violates DGCL § 141(a). Accordingly, the bylaw is void.

(A) is incorrect.

See the answer to choice B.

(C) is incorrect.

See the answer to choice B.

(D) is incorrect.

See the answer to choice B.

Answer to Question 23

(D) is the correct answer.

This question is loosely based on *Kamin v. American Express Co.*, 54 A.D.2d 654 (N.Y. 1976). Under Delaware law, corporate directors have fiduciary duties of loyalty and care. However, when they make business judgments, they are protected by the so-called business judgment rule. This means that courts will not second-guess the board's decision as long as the directors (a) were reasonably informed, (b) acted in good faith, and (c) acted without a conflict of interest. The business judgment rule effectively limits the director's fiduciary duties. In making business judgments, directors do not violate their duty of care as long as they are reasonably informed. And they do not violate their duty of loyalty, as long as they act in good faith and without a conflict of interest.

In the case at hand, nothing suggests a duty of loyalty violation. There is no indication that Peter faced a conflict of interest. Moreover, a director acts in good faith as long as he does what he honestly thinks is in the best interest of the corporation, and it is for plaintiffs to prove that the director failed to meet this requirement. In the case at hand, Peter sought to protect the corporation's stock price against an adverse reaction by the stock market, and nothing suggests that he did this for reasons other than to protect the interests of shareholders. Accordingly, we have to assume that he acted in good faith and without a conflict of interest and therefore has not violated his duty of loyalty.

What about the duty of care? As previously mentioned, a director complies with his duty of care as long as he is reasonably informed when he makes his decision. Moreover, to breach the duty of care, a director has to act with gross negligence (*Aronson v. Lewis*, 473 A.2d 805, 812 (Del. 1984)). In the case at hand, Peter was fully aware of the adverse tax consequences of his decision, and was therefore reasonably informed when he made his choice. Accordingly, he has not violated his duty of care. Note, in this context, that the business judgment rule can lead to somewhat counterintuitive results with respect to the duty of care. When a director simply overlooks the potential adverse consequences of his decision, he may violate the duty of care if his sloppiness rises to the level of gross negligence. By contrast, if the director knows about the adverse consequences and then absurdly chooses to go through with the relevant decision anyway, his decision is protected by the business judgment rule as long as he also acted in good faith and without a conflict of interest.

(A) is incorrect.

See the answer to choice D.

(B) is incorrect.

See the answer to choice D.

(C) is incorrect.

See the answer to choice D.

Answer to Question 24

(C) is the correct answer.

The business judgment rule applies only to decisions made in the absence of a conflict of interest, in good faith, and in a reasonably informed fashion. In the case at hand, Fredo failed to satisfy the business judgment rule for two reasons. First, he was not reasonably informed. And second, he had a conflict of interest. (Both Fredo and the other directors were related to Michael). Therefore, Fredo is not protected by the business judgment rule, and this would be true even if his belief that the property was worth $700,000 was based on careful and reasonable investigation. Furthermore, note that Fredo did not act in bad faith because he honestly thought the value of the property was $700,000.

(A) is incorrect.

It is true that Fredo has breached the duty of care, but he has also breached the duty of loyalty because he acted in the presence of a conflict of interest. See the answer to choice C.

(B) is incorrect.

Fredo did not act in bad faith because he honestly thought the value of the property was $700,000. See the answer to choice C.

(D) is incorrect.

Choice C is correct. See the answer to choice C.

Answer to Question 25

(A) is the correct answer.

The first question that arises is whether the suit has to be brought as a direct suit or as a derivative suit. In the landmark 2004 case *Tooley v. Donaldson*, 845 A.2d 1031, 1033 (Del. 2004), the Delaware Supreme Court drew the line between direct suits and derivative suits as follows:

"That issue must turn solely on the following questions: (1) who suffered the alleged harm (the corporation or the suing stockholders, individually); and (2) who would receive the benefit of any recovery or other remedy (the corporation or the stockholders, individually)?"

In the case at hand, it is the corporation that suffered the harm (a monetary loss resulting from the too-low sales price). Moreover, the corporation would have to receive the benefit of recovery, because if the corporation is paid damages, both the corporation's loss and the shareholders' loss (which turns on the corporation's loss) are eliminated. It follows that the suit has to be brought as a derivative suit.

For derivative suits (but not for direct suits), Chancery Court Rule 23.1 imposes a demand requirement, providing that "[t]he complaint shall . . . allege with particularity the efforts, if any, made by the plaintiff to obtain the action the plaintiff desires from the directors or comparable authority and the reasons for the plaintiff's failure to obtain the action or for not making the effort." However, no demand needs to be brought if such a demand would be futile. In making that determination, Delaware courts generally apply the so-called Aronson-test. In *Brehm v. Eisner*, 746 A.2d 244, 256 (Del. 2000), the Delaware Supreme Court summarized this test as follows:

"The test of demand futility is a two-fold test under Aronson and its progeny. The first prong of the futility rubric is 'whether, under the particularized facts alleged, a reasonable doubt is created that . . . the directors are disinterested and independent.' . . . The second prong is whether the pleading creates a reasonable doubt that 'the challenged transaction was otherwise the product of a valid exercise of business judgment.' . . . These prongs are in the disjunctive. Therefore, if either prong is satisfied, demand is excused."

Note that the first prong refers to the time that the suit is brought, whereas the second prong refers to the time of the challenged transaction. It is also worth noting that the first prong is satisfied as long as the particularized facts alleged by the plaintiff create reasonable doubt regarding the disinterestedness of a *majority* of the directors. In other words, the fact that a minority of directors are disinterested at the time the suit is brought does not prevent the plaintiff from invoking the futility doctrine.

In the case at hand, demand was futile under both prongs. The plaintiff can create reasonable doubt regarding the board's disinterestedness and independence at the time the suit is brought because there is nothing in the case to suggest that any of the directors involved in the transaction have been replaced, and every single one of the directors has a conflict of interest. Moreover, the challenged transaction also failed to satisfy the business judgment rule (both because the board was not reasonably informed and because every single director had a conflict of interest). Therefore, demand was futile.

(B) is incorrect.

Demand will be excused due to futility. See the answer to choice A.

(C) is incorrect.

Luca has to bring a derivative suit rather than a direct suit. See the answer to choice A.

(D) is incorrect.

Luca has to bring a derivative suit rather than a direct suit. See the answer to choice A.

Answer to Question 26

(D) is the correct answer.

DGCL § 102(b)(7) provides that a corporation's charter can contain a provision eliminating or limiting the liability of a director for fiduciary duty violations, but such a provision cannot eliminate or limit the liability for duty of loyalty violations. In other words, if a corporation's certificate of incorporation eliminates the directors' liability for fiduciary duty violations "to the fullest extent permitted by law," then the director has nothing to fear if he has solely breached duty of care by failing to be reasonably informed. By contrast, he remains liable if he has breached his duty of loyalty by acting in bad faith or in the presence of a conflict of interest. This said, in the case at hand, there is no indication that Fredo has acted in bad faith or that he faced a conflict of interest. His only fault was a failure to be reasonably informed. Hence, the exculpation clause protects Fredo from any liability regarding the sale of the Villa.

(A) is incorrect.

Fredo did not violate his duty of loyalty. See the answer to choice D.

(B) is incorrect.

The sale did not constitute a distribution. A distribution occurs where assets are transferred from the corporation to a shareholder in his capacity as a shareholder. There is no indication that Max owned any shares in the corporation, and even if he did, there is nothing to suggest that the sale had anything to do with Max being a shareholder.

(C) is incorrect.

DGCL § 102(b)(7) allows for provisions that limit or eliminate the liability of directors for duty of care violations; and in the case at hand, Fredo only violated his duty of care, not his duty of loyalty. See the answer to choice D.

Answer to Question 27

(D) is the correct answer.

Paul has not violated any fiduciary duties. The reason is quite simple. Paul is a minority shareholders and, as a general rule, minority shareholders do not have fiduciary duties under Delaware law.

In answering this question, many students tend to apply the corporate opportunity doctrine. Under that doctrine, corporate fiduciaries such as officers and directors are, in principle, required to abstain from exploiting business opportunities that belong to the corporation. This doctrine is rooted in the duty of loyalty. Under Delaware case law, a controlling shareholder has fiduciary duties to the corporation. Therefore, a controlling shareholder can potentially violate his duty of loyalty by exploiting opportunities belonging to the corporation. However, Paul is not a controlling shareholder and therefore does not have a duty of loyalty, making the corporate opportunity doctrine inapplicable.

(A) is incorrect.

See the answer to choice D.

(B) is incorrect.

See the answer to choice D.

(C) is incorrect.

If the corporate opportunity doctrine were applicable to this case, then the question of whether Paul represented the opportunity to the right person would indeed be relevant. Under Delaware law, a fiduciary is at liberty to exploit a corporate opportunity once he has presented it to the board and the board has rejected it after full disclosure of all pertinent facts. By contrast, presenting a corporate opportunity to the corporation's CEO is not per se sufficient, even if the CEO rejects the relevant opportunity. Hence, if this case were governed by the corporate opportunity doctrine, presenting it to Christine would not per se suffice to allow Paul to exploit the relevant opportunity. However, as explained in the answer to choice D, the corporate opportunity doctrine does not even apply to this case because Paul does not owe a duty of loyalty to the corporation. Therefore, the causal relationship ("because") asserted by answer choice C is incorrect.

Answer to Question 28

(D) is the correct answer.

The duty of loyalty requires directors to act in what they perceive to be the best interest of the corporation. Moreover, it is for the plaintiff to prove that a director has violated his duty of loyalty. In the case at hand, there is no indication whatsoever that Carl failed to act in what he perceived to be the best interest of the corporation. In particular, the facts specifically state that Carl thought the car was worth $2000. Hence, Carl has not violated his duty of loyalty.

What about the fact that the car was worth less than Carl thought it was. Note, first, that the consideration for which shares are issued does not have to consist of cash. Rather, under DGCL § 152, "[t]he board of directors may authorize capital stock to be issued for consideration consisting of cash, any tangible or intangible property or any benefit to the corporation, or any combination thereof." Hence, issuing shares in exchange for a used car is entirely permissible. Moreover, "[i]n the absence of actual fraud in the transaction, the judgment of the directors as to the value of such consideration shall be conclusive," DGCL § 152. Under Delaware case law, "[m]ere inadequacy of price, unless so gross as to lead the court to conclude that it was due not to an honest error of judgment but rather to bad faith or to a reckless indifference to the rights of others interested, will not reveal fraud," (*Fidanque v. American Maracaibo Co.,* 92 A.2d 311, 321 (Del. Ch. 1952)). In the case at issue, Carl has made an honest mistake rather than committed fraud. Accordingly, his judgment as to the value of the car is conclusive.

(A) is incorrect.

See the answer to choice D.

(B) is incorrect.

See the answer to choice D.

(C) is incorrect.

See the answer to choice D.

Answer to Question 29

(B) is the correct answer.

Note, first, that under DGCL § 153(a), "[s]hares of stock with par value may be issued for such consideration, having a value not less than the par value thereof, as determined . . . by the board of directors." In other words, the par value determines the minimum value of the consideration for which a par value share may be issued. In the case at hand, the value of the consideration, as determined by the board, was lower than the par value, rendering the transaction illegal. Note that no violation against DGCL § 153(a) would have occurred if the par value of the share had been $400.

As regards the possibility of issuing shares in exchange for unsecured promissory notes, the law has changed over time. Until 2004, Delaware's Constitution imposed a requirement that "[n]o corporation shall issue stock, except for money paid, labor done or personal property, or real estate or leases thereof actually acquired by such corporation." (Del. Const. Art. IX, § 3). Not surprisingly, the Delaware Supreme Court held that an unsecured promissory note did not qualify as "actually acquired" consideration with the consequence that stock issued in exchange for an unsecured promissory note was voidable at the election of the corporation (*Lofland v. Cahall*, 118 A. 1, 4 (Del. 1921)). However, in 2004, the relevant provision was deleted from the Delaware Constitution. Now, DGCL § 152 makes it clear that "[t]he board of directors may authorize capital stock to be issued for consideration consisting of cash, any tangible or intangible property or any benefit to the corporation, or any combination thereof." It follows that issuing stock in exchange for an unsecured promissory note is now entirely legal.

(A) is incorrect.

See the answer to choice B.

(C) is incorrect.

See the answer to choice B.

(D) is incorrect.

See the answer to choice B.

Answer to Question 30

(B) is the correct answer.

The bylaw classifying the board is in fact void. According to DGCL § 141(d), the board can be classified, but only "by the certificate of incorporation or by an initial bylaw, or by a bylaw adopted by a vote of the stockholders." In the case at hand, the corporation was formed back in 1925, so classifying the board via an initial bylaw is no longer an option. Accordingly, the only options now available are classification via the certificate of incorporation and classification via shareholder-adopted bylaw.

(A) is incorrect.

It is true that the board can be classified by amending the certificate of incorporation. According to DGCL § 141(d), the board can be classified "by the certificate of incorporation or by an initial bylaw, or by a bylaw adopted by a vote of the stockholders."

(C) is incorrect.

It is true that the board can be classified via a shareholder-adopted bylaw, DGCL § 141(d). Moreover, the fact that the corporation's certificate of incorporation explicitly authorized the board to amend, repeal, or adopt bylaws does not prevent the shareholders from adopting a bylaw classifying the board. Under the legal default, the corporation's shareholders have the power to adopt, amend, or repeal bylaws, DGCL § 109(a). Furthermore, even where—as in the present case—the certificate of incorporation empowers the board to adopt, amend, or repeal bylaws, the shareholders still retain their power to adopt, amend, or repeal bylaws as well, DGCL § 109(a).

(D) is incorrect.

(D) is incorrect because (B) is the correct answer.

Answer to Question 31

(B) is the correct answer.

Under DGCL § 271, the board's decision to "sell, lease or exchange all or substantially all" of its property or assets has to be approved by a majority of the outstanding stock of the corporation entitled to vote thereon. The only question, therefore, is whether the factory constitutes "all or substantially all" of the corporation's assets.

In the past, Delaware courts defined the term "all or substantially all" extremely broadly. In one case, *Katz v. Bregman*, 431 A.2d 1274 (Del. Ch. 1981), the Court went so far as to apply DGCL § 271 despite the fact that the assets that were sold represented only about 51% of the corporation's assets and accounted for only about 52% of its pre-tax net operating income. However, in the 2004 case *Hollinger v. Hollinger International*, 858 A.2d 342, 385 (Del. Ch. 2004), the Delaware Chancery Court returned to a much more restrictive interpretation of DGCL § 271. The Court made it clear that "substantially all" means "substantially all" and that DGCL § 271 therefore cannot be applied where the assets that remain are both substantial and viable. Against this background, DGCL § 271 presumably applies where the factory constitutes 95% of the corporation's business, especially given that the remaining assets are not profitable. By contrast, if the factory had constituted only 50% of the corporation's assets and if the remaining parts had been profitable, then DGCL § 271 would not have applied.

(A) is incorrect.

See the answer to choice B.

(C) is incorrect.

See the answer to choice B.

(D) is incorrect.

See the answer to choice B.

Answer to Question 32

(B) is the correct answer.

For derivative suits (but not for direct suits), Chancery Court Rule 23.1 imposes a demand requirement, providing that "[t]he complaint shall . . . allege with particularity the efforts, if any, made by the plaintiff to obtain the action the plaintiff desires from the directors. . . ." However, no demand needs to be brought if such a demand would be futile. In making that determination, Delaware courts generally apply the so-called Aronson test. This test has two prongs, and demand is considered futile if at least one of these prongs is satisfied.

Under the first prong, demand is futile if the plaintiff has alleged particularized facts that create reasonable doubt whether, at the time the suit is brought, the directors are disinterested and independent. The underlying idea is that it makes no sense to ask the board to sue on behalf of the corporation if the board cannot be expected to make that decision in a disinterested manner. Importantly, for this prong to be satisfied, the plaintiff only needs to create reasonable doubt regarding the disinterestedness and independence of a majority of the directors. Hence, the fact that a minority of the directors are disinterested and independent does not make the derivative suit inadmissible.

Under the second prong, the plaintiff's pleading has to create a reasonable doubt that the challenged transaction satisfied the business judgment rule. The underlying idea is that if the challenged transaction failed to satisfy the business judgment rule, then the directors may face personal liability and therefore cannot be expected to act impartially in deciding whether or not to bring suit on behalf of the corporation.

If one were to apply the Aronson test to the situation at hand, the derivative suit would be admissible. That is because the challenged transaction clearly failed the business judgment rule. The sale of the property to Tim was a self-dealing transaction in which four of the five directors faced a clear conflict of interest.

However, there are some situations in which the Aronson test does not apply. These situations have in common that despite the fact that the challenge transaction flunked the business judgment rule, the corporation's board can be expected to make a disinterested decision about whether or not to sue at the time that the derivative suit is filed. In *Rales v. Blasband* (634 A.2d 927, 933–34 (Del. 1993)), the Delaware Supreme Court summarized the relevant legal principles as follows:

"Consistent with the context and rationale of the *Aronson* decision, a court should not apply the *Aronson* test for demand futility where the board that would be considering the demand did not make a business decision which is being challenged in the derivative suit. This situation would arise in three principal scenarios: (1) where a business decision was made by the board of a company, but a majority of the directors making the decision have been replaced; (2) where the subject of the derivative suit is not a business decision of the board; and (3) where . . . the decision being challenged was made by the board of a different corporation."

If any of the three situations described above is given, demand is futile only if the plaintiff alleges particularized facts creating doubt regarding the disinterestedness of a majority of the directors at the time the suit is filed. In other words, in those cases, demand futility requires that the first prong of the Aronson test is satisfied. In the case at hand, this requirement is not met. A majority of the directors had in fact been replaced after the challenged transaction, and, at the time the derivative suit is filed, more than half of the directors had no conflict of interest and where not involved in the challenged transaction. Therefore, demand is not excused, and the derivative suit is inadmissible.

By contrast, there is no reason to think that Jill cannot fairly and adequately represent the interests of the other shareholders. Essentially, this requirement is met as long as there is no obvious conflict of interest between the plaintiff and the other stockholders, and, in the case at hand, nothing suggests a conflict of interest.

(A) is incorrect.

See the answer to choice B.

(C) is incorrect.

See the answer to choice B.

(D) is incorrect.

See the answer to choice B.

Answer to Question 33

(A) is the correct answer.

For derivative suits (but not for direct suits), Chancery Court Rule 23.1 imposes a demand requirement. However, that does not imply that making such a demand before bringing suit is a good idea. If the plaintiff makes a demand on the corporation, and the board of the corporation decides not to bring suit, then that decision is, in principle, protected by the business judgment rule (*Zapata v. Maldonado*, 430 A.2d 779, 784 n.10 (Del. 1981)). Even worse, by making the demand, the shareholder has, in effect, conceded that the board is disinterested and independent. Consider the following excerpt from *Spiegel v. Buntrock* (571 A.2d 767, 777 (Del. 1990)):

"Whenever any action or inaction by a board of directors is subject to review according to the traditional business judgment rule, the issues before the Court are independence, the reasonableness of its investigation and good faith. By electing to make a demand, a shareholder plaintiff tacitly concedes the independence of a majority of the board to respond. Therefore, when a board refuses a demand, the only issues to be examined are the good faith and reasonableness of its investigation."

As a result, once a demand has been made, the shareholder cannot sue on behalf of the corporation unless he can show that the board, in refusing to sue, acted in bad faith or without being reasonably informed. Note that the burden of proof is on the plaintiff.

Note that the *Spiegel* approach has the perverse consequence of giving plaintiffs a strong incentive not to make a demand on the corporation before bringing suit, because it is much easier to argue that demand was futile than to show that the board acted in bad faith or without being properly informed in rejecting a demand to bring suit.

(B) is incorrect.

See the answer to choice A.

(C) is incorrect.

See the answer to choice A.

(D) is incorrect.

See the answer to choice A.

Answer to Question 34

(B) is the correct answer.

For derivative suits (but not for direct suits), Chancery Court Rule 23.1 imposes a demand requirement. No demand needs to be brought if such a demand would be futile. However, even if demand is found to be futile, that is not the end of the story. Rather, the corporation may still be able to get the suit dismissed with the help of a special litigation committee. The leading case is *Zapata v. Maldonado*, 430 A.2d 779 (Del. 1981). There the Delaware Supreme Court held that if a court is faced with a request by a special litigation committee to dismiss a derivative suit, the court has to apply a two-step test (id. at 788). First, the litigation committee's decision has to satisfy all three requirements of the business judgment rule: good faith, reasonable information, and disinterestedness. Crucially, it is the corporation—rather than the plaintiff—that has to prove that these requirements are met. Second, even if the business judgment rule requirements are satisfied, the court will not necessarily dismiss the derivative suit. Rather, the court will then apply its own business judgment to decide whether the continuation of the litigation serves the best interest of the corporation. Answer choice B summarizes these principles and is therefore correct.

(A) is incorrect.

As a general rule, the burden of proof regarding the elements of the business judgment rule is on the plaintiff. However, that allocation of the burden of proof no longer applies when a litigation committee asks the court to dismiss an admissible derivative suit. In that situation, it is the corporation that has to prove that the committee's decision satisfies the elements of the business judgment rule. See the answer to choice B.

(C) is incorrect.

This answer choice is incorrect for two reasons. First, when a special litigation committee asks the court to dismiss an admissible derivative suit, the burden of proof regarding the elements of the business judgment rule is on the corporation. See the answer to choice A. And second, even if the court comes to the conclusion that the elements of the business judgment rule are satisfied, it will not dismiss the derivative suit automatically. Rather, the court will use its own business judgment to determine whether the continuation of the derivative suit lies in the interest of the corporation. See the answer to choice B.

(D) is incorrect.

Rather than dismissing the suit automatically, the court will use its own business judgment to determine whether the continuation of the suit lies in the corporation's best interest. See the answer to choice B.

Answer to Question 35

(D) is the correct answer.

Steven can be held liable if he has violated his fiduciary duties. Directors can violate their fiduciary duties by failing to monitor the corporation's business in an appropriate manner. However, it is very important in this context to distinguish between the duty of care and the duty of loyalty.

In order for the duty of loyalty to be breached, the director's failure to monitor must rise to the level of bad faith. For example, a director who simply decides not to exercise his duties anymore, thereby "abandoning" his office, violates his duty of loyalty. Similarly, a director who is aware of an employee's wrongdoing but fails to step in because he has become indifferent to the corporation's fate, acts in bad faith. By contrast, mere negligence or stupidity does not constitute bad faith. Accordingly, Steven has not breached his duty of loyalty.

Even if a failure to monitor does not breach a director's duty of loyalty, it may still constitute a breach of the duty of care. The duty of care can be violated for one of two reasons. First, a director violates his duty of care if he ignores obvious danger signs ("red flags") that should have alerted him to possible wrongdoing. It must be kept in mind that a violation of the duty of care requires gross negligence. Second, corporations are expected to have in place a "system of watchfulness" that will allow their directors to become informed about employee wrongdoing. Having no such system in place constitutes a violation of the duty of care.

Even if a director has violated his duty of care, he may not be liable to the corporation. A corporation's certificate of incorporation may contain a clause limiting or eliminating a director's liability for violations of the duty of care. If the certificate of incorporation contains a liability waiver for duty of care violations, then a director's failure to monitor only exposes him to personal liability if it rises to the level of a duty of loyalty violation.

Answer choices A, B, and C do not apply these principles correctly. See answers to choices A, B, and C.

(A) is incorrect.

Steven violated his duty of care regardless of whether the corporation had in place a system of watchfulness. The duty of care does not only require corporate directors to make sure that the corporation has in place some system of watchfulness to ferret out employee wrongdoing. Rather, directors also violate their duty of care by ignoring obvious danger signs. This is what Steven did when he brushed aside both the information about Catherine's gambling and Bill's report about possible accounting inaccuracies. Hence, Steven can be held personally liable. See the answer to choice D.

(B) is incorrect.

Steven did not act in bad faith, because he did not know that Catherine was stealing from the corporation. Mere stupidity does not amount to bad faith. See the answer to choice D.

(C) is incorrect.

Under DGCL § 141(e), directors can rely in good faith on reports that the corporation's employees present to the corporation. However, this principle does not allow directors to ignore obvious red flags pointing to employee wrongdoing.

Answer to Question 36

(D) is the correct answer.

Long form mergers are governed by DGCL § 251. As a general rule, a long form merger has to be approved by the shareholders of both companies, DGCL § 251(c). Admittedly, there exists an exception to this rule. Under DGCL § 251(f), if the merger is a relatively unimportant transaction for one of the companies involved, the shareholders of that company do not have to approve the merger. However, that exception requires inter alia, that the relevant corporation is the corporation that survives the merger. In the case at hand, Big Corp. did not survive the merger, and, accordingly, the approval of Big Corp.'s shareholders cannot be rendered unnecessary by DGCL § 251(f).

But what if the transaction was structured as a so-called short-form merger? Short-form mergers are governed by DGCL § 253. A short form merger is only possible in those cases where one of the corporations holds 90% or more of the outstanding shares of the other corporation, DGCL § 253(a). As a general rule, a short form merger does not have to be approved by the shareholders of either of the corporations involved, DGCL § 253(a). However, there exists an important exception to this rule. If the parent corporation does not survive the merger, then the merger requires the approval of the parent corporation's shareholders, DGCL § 253(a). In the case at hand, this exception is applicable, because Big Corp. is the parent corporation, and Big. Corp. does not survive the merger. Hence, the merger has to be approved by Big Corp.'s shareholders.

(A) is incorrect.

See the answer to choice D.

(B) is incorrect.

See the answer to choice D.

(C) is incorrect.

See the answer to choice D.

Answer to Question 37

(C) is the correct answer.

Because Gold Corp. already owns 90% of Silver Corp.'s shares, the merger can be undertaken as a so-called short form merger under DGCL § 253. A short form merger under DGCL § 253 does not require the approval of the shareholders of the subsidiary corporation. Hence, in a short form merger, the minority shareholders of the subsidiary do not get to vote on the merger, and that is true regardless of whether the subsidiary corporation (Silver Corp.) or the parent corporation (Gold Corp.) is the surviving corporation.

(A) is incorrect.

See the answer to choice C.

(B) is incorrect.

See the answer to choice C.

(D) is incorrect.

See the answer to choice C.

Answer to Question 38

(D) is the correct answer.

In order for George to be entitled to appraisal, two conditions must be met. First, appraisal rights have to be available, cf. DGCL § 262(b). And second, he must have complied with the relevant procedural and other requirements in DGCL § 262(a) and (d).

According to DGCL § 262(b), appraisal rights are generally available in case of a long form merger under DGCL § 251. However, there are exceptions to this rule. Inter alia, under DGCL § 262(1)(a), no appraisal rights are available if the shares for which appraisal is sought were listed on a national securities exchange. But there is a counter-exception to the exception. According to DGCL § 262(1)(a), appraisal rights are available after all, if under the merger agreement, the shareholder receives anything for his shares other than certain types of consideration. Crucially, cash is one of the "approved" types of consideration, but only if it is received "in lieu of fractional shares."

For example, if the merger agreement had provided that every Gold Corp. shareholders receives one share in the surviving corporation for every two shares in the old corporation and—if the shareholder holds an uneven number of shares—$1000 for the remaining "odd" share, then appraisal would not be available. But in the case at hand, the merger agreement provides that the Gold Corp. shareholders get cash for all of their Gold Corp. shares rather than merely for fractional shares. Accordingly, appraisal rights are available.

The question remains, though, whether George has also met the procedural requirements imposed by DGCL § 262(a) and (d). As demanded by DGCL § 262(a), George has neither voted for the merger nor consented to the merger in writing. Moreover, he has held his shares throughout the merger. And as required by DGCL § 262(d)(1), George sent the corporation a written demand for appraisal before the vote on the merger. Moreover, he made a written demand for appraisal after the meeting. Note that such a request must be made within 20 days after the corporation has notified the shareholders that appraisal rights are available, see DGCL § 262(d). George made his written demand in a timely fashion. Therefore, George is entitled to appraisal.

(A) is incorrect.

See the answer to choice D.

(B) is incorrect.

See the answer to choice D.

(C) is incorrect.

Under DGCL § 262(a), a shareholder is entitled to appraisal only if he has complied the requirements of DGCL § 262(d). If George had not notified Gold Corp. before the merger vote of his demand for appraisal, then he would not have complied with DGCL § 262(d)(1), and therefore, he would not be entitled to appraisal. See the answer to choice D.

Answer to Question 39

(D) is the correct answer.

Shareholders in closely held corporations are notoriously vulnerable to exploitation by controlling shareholders or controlling groups of shareholders. Often the corporation fails to pay dividends such that the shareholders can only obtain money from the corporation by working for the corporation. Yet sometimes, the controlling shareholder or shareholders use their clout to make sure that they are the only ones obtaining such employment. To help minority shareholders in such a situation, states have taken different approaches.

Some states have adopted so-called oppression statutes. These statutes allow courts to dissolve the corporation at the request of a minority shareholder, if the minority shareholder or shareholders are being oppressed by those in control. Other states impose strong partnership-style fiduciary duties on shareholders in a closely held corporation. The underlying idea is that in terms of their governance, closely held corporations are really more akin to partnerships than to public corporations. In states with partnership-style fiduciary duties, the corporation may have to treat its shareholders equally unless it can show a legitimate reason for disparate treatment (*Wilkes v. Springside Nursing Home, Inc.*, 353 N.E.2d 657 (Mass. 1976)). Some states have even adopted both approaches, combining partnership-style fiduciary duties with oppression statutes. On the other hand, there are also states that have not adopted any special protections for shareholders in closely held corporations, and Delaware is one of these states. In other words, Delaware has neither adopted partnership-style fiduciary duties nor has Delaware enacted a so-called oppression statute.

(A) is incorrect.

See the answer to choice D.

(B) is incorrect.

See the answer to choice D.

(C) is incorrect.

See the answer to choice D.

Answer to Question 40

(D) is the correct answer.

Control of a corporation is valuable. For that reason, a controlling stake in a corporation is typically sold at a higher price per share than the price paid for individual shares. In other words, the seller of a controlling stake typically receives a so-called control premium when he sells his controlling stake. The question, then, is whether he can keep this premium for himself or whether he has to share it with the corporation and/or the other shareholders.

Under Delaware law, the general principle is that the seller of a controlling stake can keep the entire control premium for himself. Thus Delaware law has never embraced the position taken by the famous case *Perlman v. Feldman*, 219 F.2d 173 (2d Cir. 1955), which, based on a very idiosyncratic set of facts, came to the conclusion that the sale of a controlling stake at a premium amounted to the appropriation of a corporate opportunity with the result that the seller had to share the premium.

The Williams Act takes a different approach, but only with respect to tender offers. In case of a tender offer, the acquirer has to buy shares pro rata from all shareholders willing to sell, and he has to buy those shares at the same price. However, the Williams Act requires a tender offer, and, in the case at hand, Alexandra bought the shares from George in a so-called private transaction. Therefore, the Williams Act does not apply.

Moreover, this case does not justify the application of the so-called looting doctrine. The looting doctrine, as applied by Delaware courts, concerns the requirements of the duty of care in the context of a sale of control: "[W]hen the circumstances would alert a reasonably prudent person to a risk that his buyer is dishonest or in some material respect not truthful, a duty devolves upon the seller to make such inquiry as a reasonably prudent person would make, and generally to exercise care so that others who will be affected by his actions should not be injured by wrongful conduct," *Harris v. Carter*, 582 A.2d 222, 234–35 (Del. Ch. 1990). If the seller fails to fulfill that duty, he may be liable for damages. However, in the case at hand, nothing suggests that Alexandra was dishonest or had any plans to plunder the corporation. Appointing new managers and slashing the workforce are perfectly legitimate (and fairly common) steps for a buyer to take, however unpleasant they may be for the company's employees.

(A) is incorrect.

The sale of a controlling stake at a premium does not amount to the appropriation of a corporate opportunity. See the answer to choice D.

(B) is incorrect.

The Williams Act does not apply to this case for lack of a tender offer. See the answer to choice D.

(C) is incorrect.

Alexandra's plans for the corporation have nothing to do with looting. Hence, even assuming that George was aware of Alexandra's plans, one cannot apply the looting doctrine. See the answer to choice D.

Answer to Question 41

(D) is the correct answer.

See the answers to choices A, B, and C.

(A) is incorrect.

The Delaware General Corporation Law does not prescribe the type of consideration that the shareholders must be given in a long-form merger. Certain types of consideration will cause the shareholders to have appraisal rights where they otherwise would not, DGCL § 262(b)(2), but that was not the question.

(B) is incorrect.

Three of the terms, namely "scorched earth," "greenmail," and "Pac-Man," are, in fact, used to refer to antitakeover defenses. In a Pac-Man defense, the target tries to gain control of the acquirer before the acquirer can gain control of the target. In the scorched earth defense, the target company seeks to deter the hostile acquirer by making itself unattractive, e.g. by taking on much more debt. Greenmail means that the target pays the hostile acquirer to go away. By contrast, there is no antitakeover defense by the name of "black tower."

(C) is incorrect.

DGCL § 141(d) allows classified boards, but the maximum number of classes under this provision is three, DGCL § 141(d).

Answer to Question 42

(D) is the correct answer.

See the answers to choices A, B, and C.

(A) is incorrect.

The Delaware General Corporation Law does not impose an upper limit on the number of directors. Rather DGCL § 141(b) simply provides that the board of directors "shall consist of 1 or more members."

(B) is incorrect.

Under DGCL § 102(b)(1), the certificate of incorporation may contain "[a]ny provision for the management of the business and for the conduct of the affairs of the corporation, and any provision . . . limiting and regulating the powers of the corporation, the directors, and the stockholders. . . ." Accordingly, Delaware corporations are free to include in their charter a provision banning poison pills.

(C) is incorrect.

Many states have enacted so-called "constituency statutes" that explicitly authorize the board to take into account the interests of constituencies other than shareholders, either generally or at least in the context of hostile takeovers. Delaware has not enacted such a statute. However, the Delaware Supreme Court has made it clear than when the corporation decides whether or not to take defensive measures against a takeover, it is legitimate for directors to take the interests of non-shareholder constituencies into account, at least as long as the break-up, change in control, or sale of the corporation has not become inevitable. Cf. *Unocal Corp. v. Mesa Petroleum Co.*, 493 A.2d 946, 995 (Del. 1985):

"If a defensive measure is to come within the ambit of the business judgment rule, it must be reasonable in relation to the threat posed. This entails an analysis by the directors of the nature of the takeover bid and its effect on the corporate enterprise. Examples of such concerns may include: inadequacy of the price offered, nature and timing of the offer, questions of illegality, the impact on "constituencies" other than shareholders (i.e., creditors, customers, employees, and perhaps even the community generally), the risk of non-consummation, and the quality of securities being offered in the exchange."

Answer to Question 43

(D) is the correct answer.

As a general rule, the board's decisions are protected by the business judgment rule. However, antitakeover measures are inherently problematic, because in preserving the target company's independence, corporate directors can also protect their own jobs. Therefore, Delaware courts have long made it clear that antitakeover measures are subject to a somewhat stricter standard of review.

At the very least, courts will apply the so-called Unocal standard. Under this standard, a court will not apply the business judgment rule straight away, but instead begin its analysis with a preliminary inquiry. More specifically, the court will ask whether the board of the target company had reasonable grounds for believing in a threat to corporate policy or effectiveness and whether the defensive measure was reasonable in relation to the threat posed. Only if the answer to both questions is yes, will the court then proceed to review the measure under the generous business judgment rule. By contrast, if the answer to one of the questions is no, then the directors have violated their fiduciary duties by adopting the relevant defensive measures.

In some cases, however, the Court will apply an even stricter standard than the Unocal standard, namely the so-called Revlon standard. Once the Revlon standard applies, "the object no longer is to protect or maintain the corporate enterprise but to sell it to the highest bidder." (*Revlon, Inc. v. Macandrews & Forbes Holdings, Inc.*, 506 A.2d 173, 184 (Del. 1986)). So when exactly is the Revlon standard triggered? Revlon applies, "when a corporation undertakes a transaction which will cause: (a) a change in corporate control, or (b) a break-up of the corporate entity" (*Paramount Communications v. QVC Network*, 637 A.2d 34, 48 (Del. 1994)). A change in control, in this sense, occurs where the target corporation originally lacked a controlling shareholder but will have a controlling shareholder after the consummation of the transaction (*Paramount Communications v. QVC Network*, 637 A.2d 34, 43 (Del. 1994)). These conditions are met in the case at hand. Therefore, Revlon applies.

(A) is incorrect.

See the answer to choice D.

(B) is incorrect.

See the answer to choice D.

(C) is incorrect.

See the answer to choice D.

Answer to Question 44

(C) is the correct answer.

In this scenario, the so-called Revlon-standard applies. As the Delaware Supreme Court held in Paramount Communications v. QVC Network, the Revlon standard applies where "a corporation undertakes a transaction which will cause: (a) a change in corporate control; or (a) a break-up of the corporate entity." Furthermore, the Court made it clear in that decision that a change in corporate control occurs where, before the transaction, control of the corporation "is not vested in a single person, entity, or group but vested in the fluid aggregation of unaffiliated stockholders" whereas after the transaction, the corporation will have a controlling stockholder. For the Revlon standard to apply, it is sufficient that one of the two Revlon triggers (change in control or breakup) applies. In the case at hand, both factors are present. Therefore, Revlon applies.

(A) is incorrect.

See the answer to choice C.

(B) is incorrect.

See the answer to choice C.

(D) is incorrect.

See the answer to choice C.

Answer to Question 45

(A) is the correct answer.

Note, first, that it is legal for a corporate charter to include a ban on antitakeover provisions. Under DGCL § 102(b)(1), the certificate of incorporation may contain "[a]ny provision for the management of the business and for the conduct of the affairs of the corporation, and any provision . . . limiting and regulating the powers of the corporation, the directors, and the stockholders. . . ." Accordingly, Delaware corporations are free to include in their charter a provision banning antitakeover measures. Since board resolutions have to comply with valid provisions in the certificate of incorporation, the ban on antitakeover measures renders the adoption of the poison pill void.

By contrast, if it were not for the relevant charter provision, the adoption of the poison pill would be perfectly legal. In particular, the adoption of the poison pill does not violate the board's fiduciary duties. The leading case is *Unocal Corp. v. Mesa Petroleum Co* (493 A.2d 946 (Del. 1985)). There, the Delaware Supreme Court made it clear that, in principle, the business judgment rule applies to defensive actions taken by the target board. However, it also pointed out that, because of the conflict of interest that directors inevitably face when trying to preserve the independence of the target corporation, the board's actions had to pass two additional hurdles in order "to come within the ambit of the business judgment rule": The directors "must show that they had reasonable grounds for believing that a danger to corporate policy and effectiveness existed" and, in addition, the defensive measure "must be reasonable in relation to the threat posed." (*Unocal Corp. v. Mesa Petroleum Co*, 493 A.2d 946, 955 (Del. 1985)). Both requirements are applied very generously, though. For example, in order to show reasonable grounds for believing in a threat to corporate policy and effectiveness, it is sufficient for the target corporation's board to argue that it thought the company was undervalued by the market and that the bid was too low. Furthermore, Delaware courts have made it clear that the adoption of a poison pill generally constitutes a reasonable response to the threat posed by a tender offer. Hence, if it were not for the ban on antitakeover provisions in the charter, the board could have adopted the poison pill without violating its fiduciary duties.

(B) is incorrect.

See the answer to choice A.

(C) is incorrect.

See the answer to choice A.

(D) is incorrect.

See the answer to choice A.

Answer to Question 46

(B) is the correct answer.

Let us start with the question of whether George can hold the "joint venture" liable. The joint venture really turns out to be a partnership, since it is an association of two or more persons to carry on as co-owners a business for profit, UPA § 6, RUPA § 202(a). The fact that Operator Corp. and Alicia called the partnership a "joint venture" does not matter. If the conditions of UPA § 6, RUPA § 202(a) are met, a partnership is formed even if the partners have no intention of farming a partnership, cf. RUPA § 202(a).

The question, then, is whether the partnership ("joint venture") is liable to George. The debt vis-a-vis George is a contractual obligation. A contractual obligation of the partnership arises under UPA § 9, RUPA § 301 if a partner acts on behalf of the partnership in concluding a contract and has the power to bind the partnership. The contract was concluded by Operator Corp. acting through its CEO Mark. When concluding the contract, Operator Corp. was explicitly acting on behalf of the joint venture and because the joint venture is a partnership, it was acting on behalf of the partnership. Operator Corp. also had the power to bind the partnership because Operator Corp. acted with authority. Each partner has the authority to incur transactions in the ordinary course of business, and buying tables is a standard transaction for a restaurant. It follows that the "joint venture", which really is a partnership, is liable to George with respect to the $100.

Alicia and Operator Corp. are also liable to George since under UPA § 15, RUPA § 306, partners are personally liable for the debts of the partnership.

The question remains whether Mark is personally liable. This depends on whether he can be held liable for Operator Corp.'s debt, and that in turn depends on whether we can pierce the veil. However, there is no sufficient reason for veil piercing. One could argue that the corporation was undercapitalized (its assets were only $10), but undercapitalization alone is generally not thought to be a sufficient reason for piercing the corporate veil (even in tort cases). Undercapitalization plus a failure to follow corporate formalities might be enough to pierce, but as the question explicitly states "Mark always makes sure that all corporate formalities are scrupulously followed." Hence, it is highly unlikely that the veil will be pierced. It follows that George can hold the joint venture, Alicia, and Operator Corp. liable, but very probably not Mark.

(A) is incorrect.

See the answer to choice B.

(C) is incorrect.

See the answer to choice B.

(D) is incorrect.

See the answer to choice B.

Answer to Question 47

(D) is the correct answer.

Note, first, that the decision to reimburse Peter does not constitute a dividend. A dividend is a distribution made to a shareholder in his capacity as a shareholder. In the case at hand, however, the payment had nothing to do with the fact that Peter was also a shareholder of the corporation. Rather, it solely concerned him in his role as a former corporate director.

However, the decision to indemnify Peter is illegal because the corporation lacked the power to indemnify Peter to the relevant extent. To be sure, it is up the board to manage—or supervise the management of—the corporation's business, DGCL § 141(a). However, the ability of the corporation to reimburse its directors with respect to lawsuits is governed by DGCL § 145. In applying this provision, one has to distinguish very carefully between its various paragraphs.

The most far-reaching rule in DGCL § 145 is contained in paragraph (c) which under certain circumstances gives the director a right to be indemnified. If the requirements of DGCL § 145(c) are met, then that is all it takes—one does not also have to address the question of whether the corporation has the power to reimburse the director. *Waltuch v. Conticommodity Services, Inc.*, 88 F.3d 87 (2d. Cir. 1996). However, in the case at hand, the requirements of DGCL § 145(c) are not met, because Peter did not win on the merits or otherwise.

If the preconditions of DGCL § 145(c) are not met, then the director has no statutory right to be indemnified. This does not necessarily imply that the director won't be indemnified. However, in the absence of a statutory right to indemnification under DGCL § 145(c), the corporation can indemnify the director only if it has the power to do so under DGCL § 145(a) or (b). If the requirements set forth in DGCL § 145(a) or (b) are not met, then the corporation lacks the power to indemnify. And accordingly, any provision in the articles of incorporation or in a contract between the director and the corporation calling for such indemnification would be void. It is also worth noting that subsections (a) and (b) of DGCL § 145 only grant the board the *power* to indemnify, but, as a legal default, do not impose a *duty* to indemnify. Accordingly, even if the conditions of subsections (a) and (b) are met, unless the corporation has incurred a contractual or other obligation towards the director to exercise its power of indemnification in his favor, the board has to make a choice whether to indemnify or not. In exercising that choice, the board has to observe its fiduciary duties of loyalty and care.

In applying these principles to the case at hand, the first question is whether the corporation even had the power to indemnify Peter under DGCL § 145(a) or (b). DGCL § 145(a) pertains to third-party litigation, whereas DGCL § 145(b) concerns those cases in which the director is sued by a shareholder bringing a derivative suit or by the corporation. Because the case at hand concerns a derivative suit, the corporation's power to indemnify Peter is governed by DGCL § 145(b). Under that provision, indemnification is possible only if the director acted in good faith. Here, Peter acted in bad faith because he consciously put his sister's interests ahead of those of the corporation. Note, in this context, that under Delaware law, the good-faith requirement of the duty of loyalty is entirely subjective. If Peter had believed that hiring Pamela was in the best interest of the corporation, then he would not have violated the good faith requirement of the duty of loyalty, no matter how idiotic his belief.

Because Peter acted in bad faith, the corporation did not have the power to reimburse him under DGCL § 145(b). In any case, under section 145(b) of the Delaware General Corporation Law, the corporation can only indemnify the director against expenses (including attorney's fees), but not against judgments or amounts paid in settlement. Moreover, if the director has been held liable in court, then he cannot even be indemnified against his expenses "unless and only to the extent" that the court in which the suit was brought determines on application that the director is fairly and reasonably entitled to indemnity. Therefore, even if Peter had not acted in bad faith, but had been found liable on other grounds, Tom's decision would have been illegal.

(A) is incorrect.

See the answer to choice D.

(B) is incorrect.

See the answer to choice D.

(C) is incorrect.

See the answer to choice D.

Answers to Question 48

(B) is the correct answer.

Under Delaware law, the controller who sells his controlling stake in a private sale of control (a sale of control not involving a tender offer) has no general duty to share the control premium with the minority shareholders. It is also true that this principle is limited by the principle set forth in *In re Digex* decision (789 A.2d 1176 (Del. Ch. 2000)): Under DGCL § 203(a), the acquirer will sometimes need the consent of the target corporation's board if the acquirer wants to undertake a merger within three years of acquiring his stake in the target corporation (more specifically, within three years of becoming an "interested shareholder"). Under *In re Digex*, the board of the target should not give that waiver away for free but should rather try to get something in return.

However, in this case, Michelle does not need such a waiver since she acquires a stake of 91% and since, under DGCL § 203(a)(2), no waiver is required if upon "consummation of the transaction which resulted in the stockholder becoming an interested stockholder, the interested stockholder owned at least 85% of the voting stock of the corporation outstanding at the time the transaction commenced." Given that Michelle does not need a waiver from the incumbent board, there is no reason for her to share the control premium with the minority shareholders or the corporation.

(A) is incorrect.

Under DGCL § 203, the acquirer sometimes needs the approval of the incumbent board, if the acquirer wants to merge with the controlled corporation within three years. However, under DGCL § 203(a)(2) no such approval is required if the acquirer has managed to acquire 85% or more of the controlled corporation. Given that Michelle has bought a 90% stake, she will not need the incumbent board's approval.

(C) is incorrect.

Under the so-called looting doctrine, a controlling shareholder violates his duty of care if, despite obvious warning signs, he sells his controlling stake to a buyer who then proceeds to loot the corporation to the detriment of the other shareholders. Delaware courts have adopted a relatively narrow understanding of the looting doctrine, insisting that the seller may only incur liability in the case of gross negligence. However, none of this matters in the case at hand, since there are absolutely no signs that Michelle plans to plunder the corporation.

(D) is incorrect.

Even if Michelle held only 89% of the controlled corporation she could undertake a merger—namely a so-called long form merger under DGCL § 251—without first launching a tender offer. Moreover, even if she wanted to undertake a short form merger under DGCL § 253 which requires the parent corporation to hold 90% or more of the shares of the subsidiary, a prior tender offer is not absolutely necessary. For example, if Michelle held 89% of the outstanding shares of Angel Corp., she could try to purchase another 1 percent of the outstanding shares on the open market (through her broker) without launching a tender offer.

Answer to Question 49

(D) is the correct answer.

See the answers to choices A, B, and C.

(A) is incorrect.

It is not true that, in a long form merger, the merger agreement may amend the certificate of incorporation of the surviving corporation only to the extent that the merger complies with the general rules on charter amendments. Instead, DGCL § 251(e) generally allows for the merger agreement to amend the certificate, and Delaware case law clearly states that an amendment under DGCL § 251(e) does not have to comply with the general rules on charter amendments (see *Warner Communications Inc. v. Chris-Craft Industries Inc.*, 583 A.2d 962, 969–70 (Del. Ch. 1989)).

(B) is incorrect.

Under DGCL § 253(c), the certificate of incorporation of the surviving corporation in a short form merger can be changed without recourse to the general rules on charter amendments. The relevant changes simply have to be put forth in the merger resolution adopted by the parent corporation.

Obviously, the parent corporation's power to change the certificate of incorporation of the surviving corporation is potentially quite dangerous for the shareholders of the parent corporation. This is because as a general rule, the shareholders of the parent corporation are not entitled to vote on the short form merger unless the subsidiary corporation is the surviving corporation, DGCL § 253(a). The underlying idea is that if the parent corporation survives the merger, the merger is not sufficiently important for the shareholders of the parent corporation to require their approval.

However, once the parent corporation is given the power to change the certificate of incorporation, this picture changes drastically. After all, what prevents a corporation's management from abusing the rules on short form merger for the purpose of changing their corporation's certificate of incorporation without the consent of the shareholders? For example, assume that a corporation's management wants the corporation's charter to include a so-called staggered board provision that divides the board into three classes, DGCL § 141(d), and has the effect that directors can only be removed for cause, DGCL § 141(k)(1). To change the corporate charter without the shareholders' consent, the corporation's board could (1) incorporate a wholly owned subsidiary, (2) merge that subsidiary unto the parent corporation in a short form merger with the parent corporation as a surviving corporation, and (3) change the certificate of the parent corporation as part of the short form merger by including the relevant changes in the resolution of merger. To prevent this type of maneuvering, DGCL § 251(e) makes it clear that changes to the certificate of incorporation can only be made via the resolution of merger if the *subsidiary corporation* is the surviving corporation. That takes the sting out of the problem since a short form merger in which the subsidiary corporation is the surviving corporation requires the approval of the parent corporation's shareholders, DGCL § 253(a). In general therefore, the Delaware General Corporation Law ensures that a short form merger cannot be used to bring about changes to the parent corporation's certificate of incorporation without the approval of the parent corporation's shareholders.

There is, however, one exception to this rule. Under DGCL § 253(b), the resolution of merger can change the name of the surviving corporation, regardless of whether the surviving corporation is the parent corporation or the subsidiary. Moreover, because a corporation's name is set forth in the certificate of incorporation, DGCL § 102(a)(1), changing the corporation's name means changing the charter. And in those cases, where the parent corporation is the surviving corporation, this change does not require a vote by the parent corporation's shareholders. In other words, because of DGCL § 253(b), there exists a scenario in which the certificate of incorporation can be amended as part of a short form merger without a shareholder vote.

(C) is incorrect.

It is not true that changing the par value of shares always requires the unanimous consent of the par value shareholders. The general rules on changes to the certificate of incorporation, also called the charter, can be found in DGCL §§ 241, 242. Assuming that the corporation has already received payment for any of its capital stock, it is DGCL § 242 that applies. The extent to which amendments to the certificate of incorporation require shareholder approval is set forth in DGCL § 242(b). That provision imposes two types of approval requirements. First, all charter amendments must be approved by a majority of the outstanding shares entitled to vote thereon, DGCL § 242(b)(1). Second, if the charter provides for different classes of shares, then there are some cases in which a charter amendment also requires the approval of a particular class of shareholders. For example, if the charter amendment seeks to change the special rights of a particular class of shares, then the relevant amendment can only take effect if a majority of shares within that particular class are voted in favor of the amendment, DGCL § 242(b)(2). Crucially, with respect to the case at hand, changing the par value of par value shares is one case where the approval of the relevant class of shareholders is needed: under DGCL § 242(b)(2), the "holders of the outstanding shares of a class shall be entitled to vote as a class upon a proposed amendment . . . if the amendment would . . . increase or decrease the par value of the shares of such class. . ." However, this approval does not have to be unanimous. Rather, even if a charter amendment requires the approval of a particular class of shareholders (in addition to the approval by a majority of all outstanding shares), it is sufficient that a majority of the shares of that class are voted in favor of the amendment, DGCL § 242(b)(1). Accordingly, the statement that an amendment which alters the par value of the par value shares requires the unanimous consent of the par value shareholders is wrong.

Answer to Question 50

(C) is the correct answer.

The so-called shareholder proposal rule allows a shareholder, under certain conditions, to have her own proposal included in the corporation's proxy materials, provided the shareholder meets certain holding requirements and demonstrates eligibility (17 C.F.R. § 240.14a–8 = Rule 14a–8).

The Proxy Rules only apply to securities registered under § 12 of the Securities Exchange Act. That includes those securities (including shares) that are listed on a national securities exchange such as the New York Stock Exchange (Securities Exchange Act § 12(a)). In addition, a later provision of § 12 also covers all other securities that are issued by an issuer engaged in interstate commerce if the issuer has 500 shareholders or more and holds total assets of more than $10,000,000 (Securities Exchange Act § 12(g)). To be sure, § 12(g) of the Securities Exchange Act speaks of total assets exceeding $1,000,000. But the Securities Exchange Act allows the SEC to allow exceptions from the registration requirements it imposes, and the SEC has made use of the relevant provision to raise the threshold to $10,000,000, see 17 C.F.R. § 240.12g–1. In the case at hand, the corporation's shares were traded on the New York Stock Exchange, so the proxy rules are applicable.

In order to be eligible to submit a proposal, the shareholder must have continuously held "at least $2,000 in market value, or 1%, of the company's securities entitled to be voted on the proposal . . . for at least one year . . . ," Rule 14a–8(b)(1). Since Ann has owned at least $5,000 worth of shares, she easily meets this requirement. There are various other procedural requirements to be met, but the facts of the question are unclear in this respect.

Even if a shareholder proposal complies with all procedural requirements, Rule 14a–8(b)(i) lists various substantive grounds on which the corporation can exclude shareholder proposals. In particular, the corporation can exclude shareholder proposals that are improper under state law or shareholder proposals that deal with a matter relating to the company's ordinary business operations.

In determining whether a shareholder proposal is improper under state law, one provision to be taken into account is DGCL § 141(a) which reserves the management of the corporation to the board of directors (as opposed to the shareholders). Shareholder proposals that call for the shareholders to give binding instructions to the board of directors violate DGCL § 141(a) and are therefore improper under state law. However, in the case at hand, Ann did not seek a binding shareholder proposal. Rather, she sought a solution "recommending" a particular course of action, a so-called "precatory resolution." Since shareholders are free to make suggestions to the board without running afoul of DGCL § 141(a), this proposal is not improper under state law.

This leaves the question of whether Ann's shareholder proposal can be excluded on the ground that it deals with a matter relating to the company's ordinary business operations. That would be the case if it pertained to the day-to-day running of the corporation's business. However, that is not the case. Rather, the proposal aimed at a fundamental restructuring of the corporation's business.

Note, by the way, that the two grounds for exclusion have similar but distinct scopes of application. Because of DGCL § 141(a), any binding resolution that tells the board how to run the corporation's business is improper under state law; and that is true regardless of whether it pertains to day-to-day matters or to matters of fundamental importance. However, you can avoid falling afoul of DGCL § 141(a) by phrasing your proposal as a mere recommendation to the board. By contrast, shareholder proposals that deal with matters relating to the company's ordinary business operations can be excluded regardless of whether or not the shareholder aims at a binding instruction or at a mere recommendation. But this exclusionary ground can be avoided by focusing on matters that that are important enough to go beyond the company's ordinary business operations.

(A) is incorrect.

See the answer to choice C.

(B) is incorrect.

See the answer to choice C.

(D) is incorrect.

See the answer to choice C.

CHAPTER 8
LIMITED LIABILITY COMPANIES

Answer to Question 1

(A) is the correct answer.

Limited liability company statutes vary widely across states. Some statutes provide that the default is for an LLC to be manager-managed. Other statutes vest the power to manage the company in its members unless the LLC agreement calls for the company to be managed by managers. Delaware belongs to the latter group. Under DLLCA § 402, "the management of a limited liability company shall be vested in its members." However, this is only a default rule. In other words, the LLC agreement can deviate from the default and instead provide that the company is to be managed by managers, DLLCA § 402. Also, note that the owners of a limited liability company are called "members," just like the owners of a corporation are called "shareholders." Therefore, A is the correct answer.

(B) is incorrect.

The rule according to which a Delaware LLC is managed by its members is only a default rule, and the LLC agreement can instead provide for management by managers, DLLCA § 402. See the answer to choice A.

(C) is incorrect.

In Delaware, the default rule is that an LLC is managed by its members, DLLCA § 402. See the answer to choice A.

(D) is incorrect.

In Delaware, the default rule is that an LLC is managed by its members, DLLCA § 402. See the answer to choice A.

Answer to Question 2

(C) is the correct answer.

Under DLLCA § 402, Delaware LLCs are managed by their members unless the LLC agreement provides otherwise. However, the right and power to manage the company can be delegated, DLLCA § 407. Furthermore, "[u]nless otherwise provided in the limited liability company agreement, such delegation by a member or manager shall be irrevocable if it states that it is irrevocable," DLLCA § 407. Hence, Jay's delegation could not be revoked.

(A) is incorrect.

The right and power to manage the company can be delegated, DLLCA § 407. See the answer to choice C.

(B) is incorrect.

A delegation of the right and power to manage the LLC is irrevocable if the delegation states that it is irrevocable and if the LLC agreement does not provide otherwise, DLLCA § 407.

(D) is incorrect.

Under Delaware law, a member's or manager's delegation of his right and power to manage the LLC does not put an end to the member's or manager's membership in the LLC, unless the LLC agreement provides otherwise, DLLCA § 407.

Answer to Question 3

(D) is the correct answer.

Under DLLCA § 802, the Court of Chancery may, at the request of a member or manager, "decree dissolution of a limited liability company whenever it is not reasonably practicable to carry on the business in conformity with a limited liability company agreement." In the case at hand, the fact that Lake Peaceful dried up made it impracticable to continue the business in conformity with the LLC agreement, and so the Delaware Court of Chancery can dissolve the LLC. Moreover, this would be true even if Jay had not tried to steal from the company.

(A) is incorrect.

Unless otherwise provided in the LLC agreement, the death of a member does not dissolve the LLC, DLLCA § 801(b).

(B) is incorrect.

Delaware law does not give the members of a limited liability company the right to expel other members even if those other members have breached the LLC agreement. Admittedly, DLLCA § 803 explicitly mentions that the expulsion of a member does not cause the dissolution of an LLC. But this does not imply that the legal default allows for such an expulsion. Rather, it is left to the LLC agreement to provide for an expulsion right; and, as a result, no such right exists where the LLC agreement is silent.

(C) is incorrect.

The fact that the LLC's business becomes impracticable does not automatically dissolve the LLC. Rather, it is only grounds for the Court of Chancery to dissolve the LLC, DLLCA § 802. This rule makes a lot of sense. It is often difficult to tell whether an LLC's business has become impractical or not, so the involvement of the Delaware Chancery Court ensures legal certainty.

Answer to Question 4

(D) is the correct answer.

Under DLLCA § 101(7), membership can be limited to a single person. Moreover, that person can be a corporation, and that corporation does not have to be formed under Delaware law, DLLCA § 101(12).

(A) is incorrect.

See the answer to choice D.

(B) is incorrect.

See the answer to choice D.

(C) is incorrect.

See the answer to choice D.

Answer to Question 5

(C) is the correct answer.

Different state laws offer different answers to the question of whether a member can withdraw (or "resign") from a limited liability. In many states, the law recognizes such a withdrawal right, and in at least some states, the member can then demand to be paid the value of his membership, whereas in others, he does not have a right to get paid until the LLC eventually dissolves. In Delaware, however, as in many other states, the law takes a more restrictive approach. Under DLLCA § 603, "unless a limited liability company agreement provides otherwise, a member may not resign from a limited liability company prior to the dissolution and winding up of the limited liability company."

(A) is incorrect.

First, Tim could not resign from the LLC, DLLCA § 603. Second, even if the LLC agreement had provided for a right to resign such that Tim's resignation would have been effective, the resignation of a member does not cause the dissolution of the LLC, unless the LLC agreement provides otherwise, DLLCA § 801(b).

(B) is incorrect.

If Tim had in fact resigned from the LLC, then he would have had the right to be paid. According to DLLCA § 604, "any resigning member . . . is entitled to receive, within a reasonable time after resignation, the fair value of such member's limited liability company interest as of the date of resignation based upon such member's right to share in distributions from the limited liability company." However, Tim had no right to resign, DLLCA § 603, and so his resignation was not effective.

(D) is incorrect.

See the answer to choice C.

Answer to Question 6

(D) is the correct answer.

See the answers to choices A, B, and C.

(A) is incorrect.

DGCL § 1001 explicitly gives members of an LLC the right to bring derivative suits.

(B) is incorrect.

DGCL § 1003 requires the plaintiff's complaint to "set forth with particularity the effort, if any, of the plaintiff to secure initiation of the action by a manager or member or the reasons for not making the effort." In other words, while Delaware law imposes a demand requirement, such demand can be excused. In particular, no demand is necessary if the LLC's management, at the time the derivative suit is filed, cannot be expected to make a disinterested decision about whether the LLC should bring suit. In the case at hand, demand was excused because George was related to Frank and therefore faced a conflict of interest.

(C) is incorrect.

DGCL § 1003 imposes a demand requirement, making this answer choice wrong. Note that in order to be correct, answer choice C would have had to state that no demand was necessary in this particular case rather than making the more general and therefore incorrect claim that Delaware LLC law imposes no demand requirement.

Answer to Question 7

(D) is the correct answer.

See the answers to choices A, B, and C.

(A) is incorrect.

It is true that the certificate of formation must include the LLC's name, the address of the LLC's registered office, and the name and address of its registered agent, DLLCA § 201(a)(1) & (2). However, the certificate of formation may also contain "[a]ny other matters the members determine to include therein," DLLCA § 201(a)(3).

(B) is incorrect.

Delaware law—like the law of other states—distinguishes clearly between the LLC agreement and the certificate of formation. The term "LLC agreement," defined in DLLCA § 101(7), encompasses "any agreement, written, oral or implied, of the member or members as to the affairs of a limited liability company and the conduct of its business." By contrast, the certificate of formation is a document which has to be filed in the office of the Delaware Secretary of State, DLLCA § 201(a), and while the Members are free to include their entire LLC agreement in the certificate of formation, DGCL § 201(a)(3), they are not required to do so. Rather, the certificate of formation's necessary content is limited to the LLC's name, the address of the LLC's registered office, and the name and address of its registered agent, DGCL § 201(a)(1) & (2).

(C) is incorrect.

Provisions in the LLC agreement are enforceable regardless of whether they are included in the certificate of formation.

Answer to Question 8

(D) is the correct answer.

According to DLLCA § 501, "[t]he contribution of a member to a limited liability company may be in cash, property or services rendered, or a promissory note or other obligation to contribute cash or property or to perform services."

(A) is incorrect.

See the answer to choice D.

(B) is incorrect.

See the answer to choice D.

(C) is incorrect.

See the answer to choice D.

Answer to Question 9

(B) is the correct answer.

According to DLLCA § 503, if the LLC agreement is silent on the question of how profits are to be allocated among the members, then "profits and losses shall be allocated on the basis of the agreed value (as stated in the records of the limited liability company) of the contributions made by each member to the extent they have been received by the limited liability company and have not been returned." In other words, the default rule is that the value of a member's contribution determines the member's share of the profits. However, only those contributions matter that have actually been received by the LLC. Because so far, George and Peter have each contributed $1000, each member is allocated half of the profits for 2014.

(A) is incorrect.

See the answer to choice B.

(C) is incorrect.

See the answer to choice B.

(D) is incorrect.

See the answer to choice B.

Answer to Question 10

(C) is the correct answer.

According to DLLCA § 502(c), "[a] limited liability company agreement may provide that the interest of any member who fails to make any contribution that the member is obligated to make shall be subject to specified penalties for, or specified consequences of, such failure." Furthermore, DLLCA § 502(c) explicitly provides that "[s]uch penalty or consequence may take the form of reducing or eliminating the defaulting member's proportionate interest in a limited liability company." Hence, the relevant provision in the LLC agreement does not violate Delaware law. Accordingly, Peter's interest was eliminated when he failed to pay his contribution in time.

(A) is incorrect.

The relevant provision in the LLC agreement was not void. See the answer to choice C.

(B) is incorrect.

The relevant provision in the LLC agreement calls for the elimination of the member's interest in the LLC, and there is no reason to interpret this provision more narrowly than its wording suggests.

(D) is incorrect.

Since (C) is correct, it follows that (D) is incorrect.

Answer to Question 11

(C) is the correct answer.

According to DLLCA § 1101(e), the LLC agreement "may provide for the limitation or elimination of any and all liabilities for . . . breach of duties (including fiduciary duties) of a member . . . to a limited liability company or to another member . . . ; provided, that a limited liability company agreement may not limit or eliminate liability for any act or omission that constitutes a bad faith violation of the implied contractual covenant of good faith and fair dealing."

(A) is incorrect.

See the answer to choice C.

(B) is incorrect.

See the answer to choice C.

(D) is incorrect.

Since (C) is correct, it follows that (D) is incorrect.

Answer to Question 12

(C) is the correct answer.

According to DLLCA § 702, "[a] limited liability company interest is assignable in whole or in part except as provided in a limited liability company agreement." This means that a member is free to assign his interest in the LLC to a third party.

The reason for this seemingly generous rule is that such an assignment does not impose a significant burden on the LLC's other members. In particular, it must be recalled that a party's interest in an LLC is not identical to that party's membership in the LLC. Rather, as defined in DLLCA § 101(8), the term " '[l]imited liability company interest' means a member's share of the profits and losses of a limited liability company and a member's right to receive distributions of the limited liability company's assets." Accordingly, DLLCA § 702(a) makes it clear that "[t]he assignee of a member's limited liability company interest shall have no right to participate in the management of the business and affairs of a limited liability" unless the other members consent or unless the LLC agreement provides otherwise.

(A) is incorrect.

> See the answer to choice C.

(B) is incorrect.

> See the answer to choice C.

(D) is incorrect.

> Since (C) is correct, it follows that (D) is incorrect.

Table of Cases